MIXED BLESSINGS

The Pro Ecclesia Series

Books in the Pro Ecclesia series are "for the Church." The series is sponsored by the Center for Catholic and Evangelical Theology, founded by Carl Braaten and Robert Jenson in 1991. The series seeks to nourish the Church's faithfulness to the gospel of Jesus Christ through a theology that is self-critically committed to the biblical, dogmatic, liturgical, and ethical traditions that form the foundation for a fruitful ecumenical theology. The series reflects a commitment to the classical tradition of the Church as providing the resources critically needed by the various churches as they face modern and post-modern challenges. The series will include books by individuals as well as collections of essays by individuals and groups. The Editorial Board will be drawn from various Christian traditions.

TITLES IN THE SERIES INCLUDE:

The Morally Divided Body: Ethical Disagreement and the Unity of the Church, edited by Michael Root and James J. Buckley

Christian Theology and Islam, edited by Michael Root and James J. Buckley

Who Do You Say That I Am?: Proclaiming and Following Jesus Today, edited by Michael Root and James J. Buckley

What Does It Mean to "Do This"?: Supper, Mass, Eucharist, edited by Michael Root and James J. Buckley

Heaven, Hell . . . and Purgatory?, edited by Michael Root and James J. Buckley

Life Amid the Principalities: Identifying, Understanding, and Engaging Created, Fallen, and Disarmed Powers Today, edited by Michael Root and James J. Buckley

Remembering the Reformation: Commemorate? Celebrate? Repent?, edited by Michael Root and James J. Buckley

The Emerging Christian Minority, edited by Victor Lee Austin and Joel C. Daniels

Repentance and Forgiveness, edited by Matthew E. Burdette and Victor Lee Austin

What's the Good of Humanity?, edited by Victor Lee Austin and Joel C. Daniels

Hope Today, edited by Matthew E. Burdette and Victor Lee Austin

Mixed Blessings

The Theologians Who Shaped Us

Edited by

Victor Lee Austin

CASCADE *Books* • Eugene, Oregon

MIXED BLESSINGS
The Theologians Who Shaped Us

Pro Ecclesia Series 12

Cascade Books
An Imprint of Wipf and Stock Publishers
199 W. 8th Ave., Suite 3
Eugene, OR 97401

www.wipfandstock.com

PAPERBACK ISBN: 979-8-3852-2116-5
HARDCOVER ISBN: 979-8-3852-2117-2
EBOOK ISBN: 979-8-3852-2118-9

Cataloguing-in-Publication data:

Names: Austin, Victor Lee, editor.

Title: Mixed blessings : the theologians who shaped us / edited by Victor Lee Austin.

Description: Eugene, OR: Cascade Books, 2025 | Series: Pro Ecclesia Series 12 | Includes bibliographical references.

Identifiers: ISBN 979-8-3852-2116-5 (paperback) | ISBN 979-8-3852-2117-2 (hardcover) | ISBN 979-8-3852-2118-9 (ebook)

Subjects: LCSH: Theology—History. | Theologians.

Classification: BT21.3 .M59 2025 (print) | BT21.3 .M59 (ebook)

Mixed Blessings

The Theologians Who Shaped Us

Edited by

Victor Lee Austin

CASCADE *Books* • Eugene, Oregon

MIXED BLESSINGS
The Theologians Who Shaped Us

Pro Ecclesia Series 12

Cascade Books
An Imprint of Wipf and Stock Publishers
199 W. 8th Ave., Suite 3
Eugene, OR 97401

www.wipfandstock.com

PAPERBACK ISBN: 979-8-3852-2116-5
HARDCOVER ISBN: 979-8-3852-2117-2
EBOOK ISBN: 979-8-3852-2118-9

Cataloguing-in-Publication data:

Names: Austin, Victor Lee, editor.

Title: Mixed blessings : the theologians who shaped us / edited by Victor Lee Austin.

Description: Eugene, OR: Cascade Books, 2025 | Series: Pro Ecclesia Series 12 | Includes bibliographical references.

Identifiers: ISBN 979-8-3852-2116-5 (paperback) | ISBN 979-8-3852-2117-2 (hardcover) | ISBN 979-8-3852-2118-9 (ebook)

Subjects: LCSH: Theology—History. | Theologians.

Classification: BT21.3 .M59 2025 (print) | BT21.3 .M59 (ebook)

Scripture quotations marked ESV are from the ESV® Bible (The Holy Bible, English Standard Version®), copyright © 2001 by Crossway, a publishing ministry of Good News Publishers. Used by permission. All rights reserved.

Scripture quotations marked NKJV are from the Holy Bible, New King James Version, copyright © 1982 Thomas Nelson.

Contents

Contributors

Victor Lee Austin is theologian-in-residence for the Episcopal Diocese of Dallas. His most recent books are *Friendship: The Heart of Being Human* and *A Post-COVID Catechesis* (Cascade).

Frederick Christian Bauerschmidt is professor of theology at Loyola University Maryland and a deacon of the Archdiocese of Baltimore. He is the author of several books, including *Thomas Aquinas: Faith, Reason, and Following Christ* and *The Essential Summa Theologiae: A Reader and Commentary*. His book *The Love That Is God* won the 2023 Michael Ramsey Prize.

Phillip Cary recently retired from teaching at Eastern University outside Philadelphia, where he was scholar-in-residence at the Templeton Honors College. He is the author of *Augustine's Invention of the Inner Self*; *The Meaning of Protestant Theology: Luther, Augustine, and the Gospel That Gives Us Christ*; and most recently, *The Nicene Creed: An Introduction*.

Carolyn A. Chau is associate professor of theology in the department of Religious Studies at King's University College, Western University (Canada), and director of the Centre for Advanced Research in Catholic Thought at King's. Her research attends to questions at the intersection of contemporary Christian ecclesiology, ethics, mission, and secular culture. She is currently working on her second monograph, following *Solidarity with the World: Charles Taylor and Hans Urs von Balthasar on Faith, Modernity, and Catholic Mission* (Cascade).

David Luy, associate professor of systematic theology at the North American Lutheran Seminary in Ambridge, Pennsylvania, researches the historical development and modern appropriation of Reformation theology. He is the author of *Dominus Mortis: Martin Luther on the Incorruptibility of God in Christ* and has contributed to various journals and encyclopedias, including *Luther Digest*, *The International Journal of Systematic Theology*, *Modern Theology*, and *The Oxford Encyclopedia of Martin Luther*. He is currently working on a monograph exploring the fate of Christocentrism in modern theology.

Charles (Chad) Raith II is chief mission integration officer at Ascension Health and adjunct professor of Christianity at John Brown University. He has authored several books, including *Aquinas and Calvin on Romans: God's Justification and Our Participation* and *Ecumenism: A Guide for the Perplexed*, with R. Dave Nelson.

Amy C. Schifrin, president emeritus of the North American Lutheran Seminary and retired faculty member at Trinity School for Ministry, is a composer of hymnody and liturgical music as well as a frequent lecturer in the fields of liturgy, homiletics, and church music. She is a contributor to the new *Wiley-Blackwell Companion to the Liturgy*.

Preface

THE CENTER FOR CATHOLIC and Evangelical Theology was formed in 1991 by two veterans of theological disputation within the North American Lutheran ecclesial world, Carl Braaten and Robert Jenson. In founding CCET they were turning away, somewhat, from struggles within the Evangelical Lutheran Church in America in order to "set [their] sights on the future of the ecumenical church." A journal was founded, namely *Pro Ecclesia*, whose editor until recently, Phillip Cary, is a contributor to the current volume. With the words *pro ecclesia* we announce our intention to consider theology from East and West, from the early church to the contemporary world: the whole Christian tradition, rooted in the church but not restricted to any given church.

A few years ago Michael Root and I, with the blessing of the CCET board, convened by Zoom a conversation of younger scholars to ask them what their perceptions were of CCET. These scholars were from a range of ecclesial backgrounds, yet all of them were committed to their respective churches. We wanted them to help us understand better how CCET is seen today, and in particular what gifts they saw us as offering present-day churches; in other words, how today we can be *pro ecclesia*.

There was, we found, somewhat of a consensus that CCET has three elements that are rarely found together: 1) a desire to engage people from multiple denominational or confessional traditions; 2) aimed at both pastors and theologians, i.e., pastors desiring theological engagement, and theologians with care to be connected with the church; and 3) with a grounding, normative stance toward the Christian theological tradition. This last element entails being not merely reactive to current challenges/issues; it further entails engagement with the rigorous work that admits differences and is willing to find, if it does, that the differences are sharper than previously thought.

That conversation led to our soliciting the papers for this Pro Ecclesia Series volume on the theme "Mixed Blessings: The Theologians Who Shaped Us." The various authors in this volume share a basic love for the Christian tradition. They both respect and continue to learn from the theologians who are discussed herein, from Augustine, Aquinas, and Luther to Pannenberg and Balthasar. It is important to emphasize that their foundational stance toward the great tradition is not one of skepticism. Nonetheless, it is also the case that there are many flaws in the tradition, errors, omissions, even truths that proved to be seeds for future flaws. This too needs to be examined, an examination that arises from our recognition that our beloved traditions are also mixed blessings.

We asked our contributors to take a theologian who has been important to them and discuss what that theologian got wrong in the light of what he got right. The book proceeds roughly chronologically. It then concludes with a personal account of how one theologian changed his mind.

Victor Lee Austin

Not Quite What Any of Us Want Him to Be: On Augustine

By Phillip Cary

AUGUSTINE IS NOT WHO I expected him to be. In many ways, that's the story of my life—of my scholarly life, at least. I was writing a dissertation on Luther, or so I thought. It was to be on Luther's theological epistemology, his account of knowing God by believing his word, and I thought I would begin with a chapter on Augustine's semiotics, his theory of signs and words and how they signify—to provide the background for Luther's doctrine of word and sacrament. But Augustine turned out to be different than what I expected. He was not a good Lutheran. It turns out, he's not exactly a good Catholic, either. I didn't plan to make this discovery, but there it was. Augustine is not exactly what any of us want him to be. And then I had to write all that down and publish it and make some good people mad at me.

What did I discover? I learned, to my dismay, that Augustine was more of a philosopher than I expected—a philosopher in a deeper sense than I had expected—and that his philosophical commitments, which did not come from Scripture or Christian faith, went deeper and were more formative than I had expected. That discovery was formative for me, and much of it in a good way. In the course of exploring how deep Augustine's philosophical commitments go, I learned a lot of philosophy that I had not expected to learn. I am a philosophy professor (I only cheat and do theology as a sideline), and I am a much better philosophy professor than I would have been without Augustine. What's more, I am a better Christian, a better thinker, a more honest person because of my decades spent studying Augustine. My encounter with him has done me a great deal of good. He is a better Christian than I am, a better thinker—indeed, just plain smarter than I am—and a man of deeper integrity than I am. And he is indeed a great theologian, from whom there is an enormous amount to learn about the logic of the doctrine of the Trinity, how to speak of the person of Christ, and the depths of the doctrine of grace. Day in, day out, year in, year out, engagement with a mind and heart like Augustine's does a body good, theologically, philosophically, and ethically. It did *me* good, studying this father of mine in the faith.

And yet, it started with a disagreement. Or at least the decades of scholarship started there, with the dismay that Augustine was not what I expected, not what I *wanted* him to be. It's a disagreement that I'm still trying to explain, to myself and others, and that's what I'm doing here.

The Powerlessness of External Things

What's the disagreement about? I came to Augustine because I wanted to understand the background to Luther's concept of the word of God, and especially Luther's notion that the gospel is like a sacrament because it has the power to give what it signifies to those who receive it properly in faith. This Catholic sacramental notion seems to me to be at the heart of the Protestant notion of the saving power of the word of God—so I figured that was an interesting topic to investigate in a dissertation. And I realized that Augustine could help me in this investigation, because it was Augustine who taught the West to think of both words and sacraments as signs, external things that signify other things, including inner things such as the gift of divine grace. So I was thinking: Augustine's theory of signs would help me understand Luther's doctrine of the word, which like all words is an external sign, but like a sacrament is capable of giving what it signifies to those who believe, including inner grace and salvation. And that way I'd get a better grasp of the Augustinian and Catholic roots of Protestant theology.

As the old Augustinian definition puts it—not quite in Augustine's exact words, but close enough: a sacrament is an outward and visible sign of an inward and spiritual grace. What's more, the sacraments of the gospel, unlike the sacraments of the Old Testament law, not only signify an inner grace but confer it. That's the medieval notion of a sacrament that you can find in Peter Lombard and Thomas Aquinas and Martin Luther: an external sign that not only signifies but confers grace on those who properly receive it. But that's *not* Augustine's notion. Or so I discovered. That discovery is what led me, willy-nilly, to turn a dissertation on Luther into a dissertation on Augustine, and then into three books, before I finally got back to Luther's epistemology of the gospel. The basis of the discovery is in the subtitle to the third book: *The Powerlessness of External Things in Augustine's Thought*.[1] I had gone to Augustine wanting to find out how he thought an external sign could give the inner gift it signified; what I discovered is that he thought it couldn't.

Why is that? What I concluded—and what took three books to fully explicate—is that there are systematic reasons why Augustine can't say external things have the power to give an inner gift, and indeed that he doesn't *want* to say this and doesn't want us to believe any such thing. It was finding that this really was Augustine's principled view, evidenced in passage after passage in his writings, that led to my dismay. Augustine clearly was not who I wanted him to be, and for reasons that go deep into the heart of his thought.

The Spirituality of Intellectual Vision

Augustine is a Platonist. A *Christian* Platonist, of course, like many others. But a more consistent and philosophically deep Platonist than most Christians. And his Platonist philosophical convictions include a spirituality, an account of how we come to God that is also a *practice* of how we come to God, grounded on what Augustine believes is an inner *experience* of coming to God, which he understands in very Platonist terms.[2] At the heart of Augustine's Platonist spirituality is the conviction that we have an inner capacity for intellectual vision, for seeing the truth with the mind's eye. This capacity is not mere imagination. It's as different from imagination as understanding the Pythagorean theorem is from imagining a yellow chalk triangle on a blackboard. This understanding, in Augustine's Latin, is *intellectus*—the word from which we get our word "intellect," of course, and from which I am deriving the phrase "intellectual vision."

---

1. Phillip Cary, *Outward Signs: The Powerlessness of External Things in Augustine's Thought* (Oxford: Oxford University Press, 2008).

2. For Augustine's Platonism and the spirituality of intellectual vision, see Phillip Cary, *Augustine's Invention of the Inner Self: The Legacy of a Christian Platonist* (Oxford: Oxford University Press, 2000), chs. 3–5.

The intellect, the mind's capacity for understanding, is like seeing, Augustine thinks, following a long philosophical tradition that goes back to Plato. It's not seeing with the eye of the body, but rather the kind of seeing you are talking about when you come to understand the Pythagorean theorem, for example, in a flash of insight, and you say: "I *see* it! I get it now!" It is a moment of insight and intellectual joy that you experience when your mind sees an unchangeable truth. It is what our minds were made for, what *we* were made for.

When Augustine famously prays, "Our hearts are restless until they rest in Thee" at the beginning of the *Confessions* (1.1.1), this experience of intellectual vision is a foretaste of what he has in mind. It's a very partial and transient glimpse of what the Catholic tradition calls beatific vision, the seeing of God that makes us happy (*beata*) by bringing our minds to rest in the ultimate Truth that is God. For Augustine, it is the intellect's experience of seeing God as "the unchangeable Truth containing all that is unchangeably true" (*On Free Choice* 2.12.33). That's what our hearts are longing for, making us restless, because to love anything else is to cling to something perishable, something that slips through our fingers like water. It is like pouring out your soul on the sand, Augustine says, describing his excessive grief at the death of a childhood friend, a mortal human being whom he loved as if he would never die (*Confessions* 4.8.13). The only stable and ultimate happiness must be to love what is unchangeable, which can never be lost because it never perishes. Hence the only true and lasting happiness in which we can rest, as he puts it later in the *Confessions* (10.23.33), is to take joy in the Truth, the immutable and imperishable Truth that is God himself. Everything else we love should be used for the sake of enjoying that Truth, as he puts it in his treatise *On Christian Doctrine* (1.3.3—1.10.10).

This is a powerful spirituality. But notice that in spelling it out I have never mentioned Jesus Christ, and didn't really have to. What animates this spirituality of Augustine's is the experience of intellectual vision, not the Word of God incarnate. The conceptuality I've used to describe it could be approved and used by a pagan Platonist such as Plotinus, the great philosopher from whom Augustine mainly learned it. Even when Augustine uses distinctively biblical terminology—for example, when he speaks of charity as the love of God and neighbor in obedience to the twofold commandment in Scripture—he interprets its meaning in terms of this Platonist spirituality. Charity means being drawn inwardly by the power of grace to perceive God as the eternal Truth, which means (to add more Platonist conceptuality) as the supreme Good that makes us happy, and as "the Beauty of all things beautiful."[3] This language of the True and the Good and the Beautiful can be read as an abstract way of conceptualizing scriptural teachings about our redemption in Christ Jesus—I think that is normally the best way to read it when it is used by Christian theologians—but when you take Augustine's spirituality of intellectual vision seriously, as the central impetus of his thought and life, then you end up coming to a more troubling observation: the Platonist conceptuality here is defining the goal of Christian life, explaining what Christian faith is for. And that observation is at the heart of what I see as the mixed blessing that is Augustine's theology.

Christ as Way, Truth, and Inner Teacher

Consider how Augustine parses the biblical teaching that Christ is the Way, the Truth, and the Life (John 14:6). Christian life is lived in and with Christ as the head of the church, whose members derive their life in God from him. Augustine points to the head going before the members into heaven, where we will follow him. We are in transit, *in via*, on the road and on the way, and the Way is Christ himself. For as Augustine famously puts it, as man, Christ is the way, and as God, he is the Truth toward which we journey.[4] This famous formulation neatly puts my point, once you add that as divine Truth, Christ is the object of intellectual vision, which in the end is the ultimate and beatific vision. Thus the Platonist concept of intellectual vision defines the goal of the Christian life as marked out by the humanity of Christ, which is our way to God.

We can add some other elements of Augustine's Christology to enrich the picture. Consider Christ as the inner teacher, presented at the culmination of Augustine's treatise *On the Teacher* (11.38). This is Christ as the eternal Wisdom of God giving us inner illumination so that we may see intelligible truths—an illumination available not just to Christians but to all who turn their minds inward to see what is unchangeably true. All intellectual insight—including that of mathematics, for example—is seeing

3. *Confessions* 3.6.10. Compare to the very similar phrase in Plato, *Phaedo* 100d. For the convergence of biblical and Platonist conceptions of love in Augustine's spirituality, see Phillip Cary, *Inner Grace: Augustine in the Traditions of Plato and Paul* (Oxford: Oxford University Press, 2008), ch. 1.

4. *City of God* 11.2. For an in-depth analysis of this chapter as emblematic of Augustine's spirituality, see Phillip Cary, *The Meaning of Protestant Theology: Luther, Augustine, and the Gospel That Gives Us Christ* (Grand Rapids: Baker Academic, 2019), ch. 3.

by the inward light of Christ. So learning from Christ the inner teacher is not learning from Christ in the flesh, the particular man who walked the earth at a particular time and place speaking Hebrew and Aramaic, whom many people have never heard of, much less believed in. Christ in the flesh gives us external words that are heard with the ear, not inner illumination and intellectual vision which, as Augustine vividly depicts it in *Confessions* 7.10.16, requires us to turn inward, withdrawing from external things of the senses.

Christ the inner teacher, the eternal Word and Wisdom of God, is thus the source of intellectual insight for every human being, the inner light of reason that enlightens every person who comes into the world (in Augustine's Platonist reading of John 1:9), which is not yet the Word that becomes flesh and dwells among us in John 1:14. Here there opens up both sides of the mixed blessing that is Augustine's theology. To start with the blessing: Augustine makes it clear that the inner teacher is not the mediator, for as Augustine insists, quoting 1 Tim 2:5, it is "the man Christ Jesus" who is the "one mediator between God and man."[5] Why? For reasons that follow from the deep roots of the faith of Nicaea and its rejection of every form of subordinationism that treats the preexistent Word of God as somehow less than, beneath, or subordinate to God the Father. The Nicene rejection of subordinationism means that the Word that was with God in the beginning cannot, in his divine nature, be the mediator between God and creation, precisely because the eternal Word is not an intermediary kind of being, beneath God the Father but above the whole creation. So the Word is not the mediator in his divine nature but in his human nature: the man Christ Jesus. The mediator is not some third type of thing in between Creator and creature (a *tertium quid* as they say in logic) but rather a logical both/and, both Creator and creature, fully God and fully human. Augustine finds all that packed into the phrase "one mediator between God and man, the man Christ Jesus." It's brilliant, it's right, it's a wonderful clarification for our thought and faith, it's a gift to the Christian tradition by the working of the Holy Spirit in the teaching of the church father Augustine—all of the above.

But then to see why the blessing is mixed, look where that leaves us with Christ the inner teacher, who is not the mediator given to faith alone but the divine light available to every intellect in creation, on Augustine's reading. It is the nature of the intellect to see the truth by this inner light of reason; only some kind of inner blindness, sin or ignorance, blocks this

---

5. *Confessions* 10.43.68, compare to *City of God* 9.15; Cary, *Augustine's Invention*, 59.

vision. It is hard to avoid the conclusion that intellectual vision of the truth, including God as the Truth, is natural to us. And this has had profound and disruptive consequences in the Catholic tradition, whose notion of beatific vision owes so much to Augustine. For Augustine, the intellect is an inner eye created to see the truth, including the Truth that contains all unchanging truths, which is God. It seems there is nothing more natural to the intellect than to see the truth, just as there is nothing more natural to the eye than to see the light; only some kind of disease or blindness can prevent it.

So Augustine knows nothing of the later Catholic teaching that the beatific vision, the supreme vision of God that makes us eternally happy, is *super*-natural. Neither the word for "supernatural" nor the concept appears in his thinking. Augustine never teaches that the ultimate vision of God requires a supernatural elevation of our intellects above their natural capacity, as Thomas Aquinas teaches (*Summa theologiae* 1.12.5). All it requires is the inner light of Truth that is available to every mind in creation.

So I think that when Pope Pius XII intervened in the long, agonizing twentieth-century conflict among Catholic theologians concerning the supernatural, he was taking a stand against Augustine, not just against the supposedly new theology of Henri de Lubac. Pius famously wrote against "those who vitiate the true gratuity of the supernatural order by affirming that God *could not* make intellectual beings without ordering and calling them to the beatific vision."[6] For Augustine, there is no possibility of there being a rational soul, mind, or intellect—human or angelic—that is not ordered toward the vision of God as Truth. Augustine's conception of intellectual vision and his use of the metaphor of the mind's eye consistently suggests that such ordering is as essential and natural to every intellect as the orientation toward receiving light is to the bodily eye. Grace is needed to heal the eye of the mind that is blinded by sin and to restore its natural power, but not to elevate it above its own nature. On this point Augustine is not a Thomist and, if the pope is to be believed, not quite a good Catholic either. Not that the pope intended to be a critic of Augustine, of course. There were many twentieth-century Catholic attempts to make Augustine look something like a neo-Thomist, and evidently Pius XII found these attempts more convincing than I do.[7]

6. *Humani Generis*, 1950, in Denzinger-Schönmetzer, *Enchiridion Symbolorum* §2318. For a further account of the issues involved, see Cary, *Augustine's Invention*, 67–71.

7. For two important efforts along this line, see Jacques Maritain, *Degrees of Knowledge* (Notre Dame: University of Notre Dame, 1995) chapter 7; and Etienne Gilson, *The Christian Philosophy of Saint Augustine* (New York: Random House, 1960), 77–96, 105–11.

Beatific Vision Without Christ

The problems with Augustine's Platonism go further, however, and even deeper into Catholic theology. It may come as a shock, for example, when a theologian as resolutely Roman Catholic as Douglas Farrow speaks of a "Christological deficit" in Thomas Aquinas, no less, because Thomas's notion of beatific vision does not make the humanity of Christ essential to that vision.[8] I agree that this is a serious deficit in Thomas's theology, but then again, I'm Protestant. I think the problem arises because, all issues of supernatural grace aside, Thomas's notion of beatific vision is thoroughly Augustinian, which is to say, the beatific vision is pure, perfect *intellectual* vision, which means it has no place for sensible things like flesh or the human face of Jesus Christ. It is not a vision that looks like the gospel narrative of the transfiguration, and to that extent it seems to me less fully Christian than the Eastern Orthodox view.

It seems to me that Farrow too is bold enough to say this kind of thing because he is resolutely a theologian of the ascension, which is to say he keeps coming back to the central Christian teaching that the man Jesus Christ is presently enthroned at the right hand of God. Richard Bauckham has helped us see that this picture of Christ on the throne of God is at the core of early Christian faith from the beginning.[9] Before the New Testament itself came into being, Christians were the people who worshiped the exalted Christ as depicted in Ps 110:1 ("The LORD said to my Lord: sit at my right hand until I make you enemies your footstool") and in Dan 7:13–14, where the Son of Man comes on the clouds of heaven to the Ancient of Days enthroned in heaven and is given an everlasting dominion and a kingdom that will have no end. This vision of an emphatically incarnate Christ, a man rightfully sitting on the throne of God, is also at the core of the Christian doctrine of the Trinity. Farrow seems to be convinced, as I am, that this vision of Christ in glory on high is also rightly at the center of anything Christians should call "beatific vision." We await his coming in glory because we expect to see the glory of God in the human face of Jesus Christ (2 Cor 4:6).

And that in turn suggests that something is amiss with the notion of Christ in heaven being the head whose members shall follow him to be

---

8. Douglas Farrow, *Theological Negotiations* (Grand Rapids: Baker Academic, 2018), 59–62.

9. Richard Bauckham, *Jesus and the God of Israel* (Grand Rapids: Eerdmans, 2008).

where he is. The biblical and creedal picture moves in the opposite direction: we await his coming again in glory, praying for the kingdom of God to come on earth as it is in heaven. Christ has always been not so much our way to God as God's way to us, for the end of the way is not our arrival in the heavenly city but the descent of the heavenly city to earth, the new Jerusalem coming down from heaven so that God may dwell among us and be our God (Rev 21:2–3).

When Augustine speaks of our movement in the opposite direction—our ascent—it has less to do with the picture of our souls going to heaven when we die than with the original Platonic inspiration for that picture.[10] It's about our mind's eye being gradually purified of its attraction to transient things of the senses, to temporal goods rather than God as the eternal Good. It's like turning from a life in which you're chasing shadows to seek instead the clear light of the Sun. It's like the eye being gradually strengthened to see more and more of the light as it climbs up out of a dark cave where it had been accustomed to see only shadows of real things. That's the picture in Plato's allegory of the cave, the enormously influential text that gave us our most important version of the metaphor of the mind's eye. Plato's allegory lies behind Augustine's use of notions like intellectual vision, inner light, conversion, the purification of the mind's eye, and the ascent to see God.[11] This Platonic picture helps explain why the final, beatific vision is not, for Augustine, a vision of Christ incarnate. His notion of the vision of God in heaven is based on a different picture than that of Christ enthroned at the right hand of the Father. It's something much more like Plato's picture of coming to see the supreme Good, shining like the Sun with a light that can only be seen by the pure intellect that leaves behind all attachment to bodily things.

Can We Learn from Words?

This also explains why Augustine has no interest in the idea of external signs giving us the grace they signify. Words are signs, he says in his treatise

10. The picture of pure disembodied souls rising above this earth after death is Platonic (*Phaedo* 114c) and is tied to the notion of souls being purified of bodily attachments so as to have a clear vision of the truth (*Phaedo* 66a–67a).

11. The allegory of the cave is found in Plato, *Republic* 7.514a–21b. Plato's metaphor of the untrained mind's eye being dazzled and overwhelmed by the strength of the intelligible light is particularly important for Augustine, who echoes the metaphorical landscape in Plato's allegory most extensively in *Soliloquies* 1.13.23.

On the Teacher 1.2, and we use words to teach, but none of us actually learns anything from words. He literally says that: you can't learn things from words (*On the Teacher* 10.33–35). You have to see things for yourself—that's one of the key intuitions behind the notion of intellectual vision, both in Plato and in Augustine. So the most words can do is to direct your attention, telling you where to look. They serve as admonitions, Augustine says (*On the Teacher* 11.36) rather like a signpost saying: "Turn here! Look over there!" It's like all of creation in *Confessions* 10:6.9 saying, in effect: "Not me! It's not me you're looking for! Look higher! Look for him who made me!" The signs we need are admonitions that direct our attention away from themselves. They are not words we cling to as if they could give us the Truth that is God.

So words are useful, but they can't give you what you're looking for. They can't make you learn or see the truth for yourself. They can't give you salvation or grace or eternal life. They are like signposts on the road, having no power of their own to move you forward such as you might find in a vehicle or an engine or fuel or food. It's like in a math class, where you can believe what the teacher tells you, but you don't really know the thing it-self—the Pythagorean theorem, say—until you can cry out, in that moment of intellectual joy: "Aha! I see it! Now I get it!"

But now imagine a different way to use words. Not like a math class, but like your beloved making a promise: "I will always be there for you. I will never leave you nor forsake you." These are the covenantal promises of God according to Holy Scripture: "Fear not, I am with you; be not dis-mayed, for I am your God. . . . I will uphold you with my righteous right hand" (Isa 41:10 ESV). That, I take it, is the biblical way of thinking about the knowledge of God: you get to know who your beloved really is when he gives himself to you in his word, like a bridegroom promising himself to his bride and being true to his word. That's the theological epistemology I think we find in Luther as well. The gospel word is like a sacrament that gives what it signifies because it contains a promise that is like a wedding vow, a word that gives us the person of whom it speaks. "I will be with you," he says, and he will. By making that promise he gives us something external to cling to, something we can hear with our ears and cling to in our hearts—cling to as an external word that saves us and gives us eternal life in Christ.[12]

12. This is the core of my interpretation of Luther's thought in Cary, *Meaning of Prot-estant Theology*, chs. 7–8.

That is not how the knowledge of God ultimately works in Augustine. Not that Augustine is unaware of the way we come to believe things about the people we love because of what they tell us about themselves—but Augustine does not usually count this as knowledge.[13] Faith in the word of God is meant to give way to sight, which for Augustine means intellectual vision that does not need words. Even faith in the word of our friends is not ultimately necessary for knowing them, because in the end we shall be able to see each other's minds directly, Augustine teaches (picking up an idea from Plotinus the Platonist).[14]

Missing Life-Giving Flesh

If I am to sum up what I miss in Augustine, it is more than just word and sacrament, external signs that give us Christ in the flesh. It is the salvific power of Christ's flesh itself. There have been long arguments about whether Augustine teaches the real presence of Christ's flesh and blood in the Eucharist. I think he does, but the question has gotten confused and complicated because scholars have overlooked what he does not teach. Augustine believes Christ's flesh is present in the Eucharist, because that is what the church teaches, but he doesn't know where to go from there: he doesn't know how to say what it could possibly mean that Christ's body—not the church, his ecclesial body, but the human body born of Mary—is salvific. Unlike his contemporary, Cyril of Alexandria, he does not articulate a piety devoted to Christ's life-giving flesh.[15] That crucial phrase, "life-giving flesh," is a paradox, after all: in any normal form of ancient thought, it is the spirit that gives life to the flesh—or the soul that gives life to the body—not the other way around. A body without a soul is a corpse, and flesh without spirit is a dead thing. But Christ's flesh, being divine flesh, the flesh of God incarnate, gives life to both our souls and our bodies. I don't think Augustine knows how to talk about this, precisely because the eternal life he anticipates is beatific vision, the kind of pure intellectual vision that you

---

13. See the discussion of Augustine's treatise *On Faith in Things Unseen*, in Cary, *Outward Signs*, 124–26, as well as the more expansive concept of knowledge found in Augustine's later work (126–30).

14. Augustine presents this thought in several passages, including the final paragraph of *City of God* 22.29. For discussion, see Cary, *Outward Signs*, 82–83, and the passages noted in 294n2.

15. See Cary, *Outward Signs*, 244–52.

can learn about in Plato. The Bible, I think, is looking elsewhere—to God in flesh.

The flesh of Christ does have a huge role to play in Augustine's theology, for Christ as man is our way to Christ as God. But I don't think Augustine knows how to say that Christ in the flesh is how God gives himself to be known as he truly is—not just as a sign functioning like all creation to say: "Not me! I'm not what you're looking for! Look higher!" Christ in the flesh, the creature who is also the Creator, says, "Come to *me* all you who are weary and heavy laden, and I will give you rest" (Matt 11:28) and "Whoever has seen *me* has seen the Father" (John 14:9). Augustine interprets the latter as an admonition to turn from Christ's flesh, which can be seen by the eyes, to his divinity, which can only be seen by the eye of the mind. But a piety grounded in Christ's life-giving flesh, exalted to the throne of God, works differently, I think.[16]

So, in conclusion, Augustine is not really who I want him to be. Yet he remains a church father, one of *my* fathers in the faith. I suppose it's a bit like discovering that your great-great-grandfather, born in the old country, lived a life that is quite different than yours, in many ways perhaps unimaginable to you. Yet you recognize that he helped make you who you are in all sorts of good ways, and the more you learn about him, the more you become capable of being surprised by the depth of his wisdom, despite the fact that in many respects you wouldn't ever want to be like him. I'm thinking that's part of coming to a grown-up relation to your forefathers and foremothers: they're not who you expect or want them to be, yet by the grace of God they keep on surprising you with good things. Mixed blessings, but blessings indeed.

16. For Augustine's treatment of Jesus's reply to Philip's question in John 14, see Cary, *Outward Signs*, 148–51.

The Dumb Ox in the Room:
Reckoning with the Legacy of Aquinas

By Frederick Christian Bauerschmidt

"We Baptize You . . ."

WHEN YOU'RE A CATHOLIC, you learn to wince automatically whenever you see the church in the news. Many of us were wincing in early 2022, when a story hit the news of thousands of baptisms deemed invalid because they were performed by a priest who used the words "*we* baptize you . . ."—what I'll call the "we-formula"—rather than "*I* baptize you. . . ."[1] This case seemed to catch the public imagination, particularly among those (including Catholics) inclined to judge the church to be clericalist, legalistic, and overly invested in scholastic exactitude. There had been a very similar case in August 2020, which for some reason did not garner as much attention, of a deacon who had been using the we-formula for decades and whose baptisms were similarly ruled invalid. In that case, a baby baptized by the deacon in 1990 had grown up and become a priest, or at least *thought* he had become a priest. Since baptism is, as it were, the "gateway" to the other sacraments, it was determined that he had not in fact received *any* of the sacraments, and so had to be rebaptized, reconfirmed, recommuned, reordained to the diaconate, and finally reordained to the presbyterate (all in less than two weeks).[2] It was sort of the ecclesiastical equivalent of

---

1. Rachel Treisman, "An Arizona Priest Used One Wrong Word in Baptisms for Decades. They're All Invalid," National Public Radio, February 15, 2022 (https://www.npr.org/2022 /02/15/1080829813/priest-resigns-baptisms).

2. Allen H. Vigneron, "Letter to the Faithful from Archbishop Vigneron," Arch-

President Obama's inaugural do-over in the Oval Office after Chief Justice John Roberts muffed the oath of office at the public inauguration.[3]

Both of these baptism cases were a result of answers in June of 2020 by the Congregation for the Doctrine of the Faith (CDF) in response to a question regarding the validity of the we-formula. The CDF said such baptism was invalid, and gave as the pastoral remedy that people baptized in this way must be baptized again *in forma absoluta*, not conditionally.[4] This exclusion of the possibility of a conditional baptism, which is when those who may or may not have been validly baptized are baptized again with the words, "If you are not already baptized . . ." appended at the beginning of the baptismal formula, is noteworthy. It suggests that there is not the slightest shadow of a doubt that the we-formula could not validly confer baptism, not only because is it hard to imagine that a Vatican congregation would create a huge pastoral headache and trample on people's certainty about their sacramental incorporation into Christ on a whim, but also because it would be blasphemous to rebaptize without condition someone who was already baptized. You would not suggest absolute rebaptism unless you had absolute certainty. Whence derives such certainty? Seemingly from Thomas Aquinas.

In the doctrinal note accompanying the decision, the first paragraph concludes: "In this regard, St. Thomas Aquinas had already asked himself the question *utrum plures possint simul baptizare unum et eundem* [whether many people can simultaneously baptize one and the same person], to which he had replied negatively, insofar as this practice is contrary to the nature of the minister."[5] This suggests that since Thomas has already asked and answered this question, we have our answer ready to hand, which only needs a bit of unpacking. Other authorities get invoked as the note proceeds, of course: Augustine, the Council of Trent, the Second Vatican

---

diocese of Detroit, August 23, 2020 (https://www.aod.org/august-23-2020-letter-to-the-faithful-english).

3. Jeff Zeleny, "I Really Do Swear, Faithfully: Obama and Roberts Try Again," *New York Times*, January 21, 2009 (https://www.nytimes.com/2009/01/22/us/politics/22oath.html).

4. Holy See Press Office, "Responses to Questions Proposed on the Validity of Baptism Conferred with the Formula 'We Baptize You in the Name of the Father and of the Son and of the Holy Spirit,'" Vatican, June 8, 2020 (https://press.vatican.va/content/salastampa/it/bollettino/pubblico/2020/08/06/0406/00923.html).

5. Holy See Press Office, "Responses to Questions Proposed," svv "Doctrinal Note on the modification of the sacramental formula of Baptism," citing *Summa theologiae* [*ST*] 3.67.6. Thomas also addresses the question, albeit briefly, in *ST* 3.66.5.

Council, and the catechsim, but one gets the distinct impression that the heavy lifting has been already done for us by St. Thomas. As the argument of the doctrinal note unfolds, it leans heavily on Thomas's view that the sacraments are acts, not of the church or her minister, but of Christ—or, more precisely, acts of the church only in a secondary sense, as constituted as the body of which Christ is the head. Thomas notes in the article of the *Summa* cited that "a person does not baptize except as a minister of Christ and as standing in his place," an intention that the use of "we" seems opposed to.[6] Thus, the argument goes, we must avoid any implication that it is the ecclesial community, and not Christ himself working through his minister, that is the agent in the act of baptism. Spelling out what is implicit in Thomas, the doctrinal note argues that the change from singular to plural shows defective intention on the part of the minister, and obscures the unique role of the minister in the sacrament: "The minister is the visible sign that the Sacrament is not subject to an arbitrary action of individuals or of the community, and that it pertains to the Universal Church."[7]

This notion of sacraments as acts of Christ and ministers acting in the place of Christ is certainly not unique to Thomas and the Thomist tradition, but it comports well with Thomas's view of sacraments as instrumental causes[8] and suggests that the placement of Thomas at the head of the doctrinal note's brief series of arguments is not accidental. Thomas's theology of the sacramental minister seems to underlie the entire argument. But perhaps it is not simply that the authors of the doctrinal note found Thomas's sacramental theology compelling. Might it be the case that the fact that Thomas seems to have already asked and answered the question, concluding that the we-formula "annuls" the sacrament, in itself gives us the answer, even apart from any assessment of Thomas's arguments? In

---

6. *ST* 3.67.6. Translations of the *Summa theologiae* are my own. Subsequent citations will be made parenthetically in the text.

7. Holy See Press Office, "Responses to Questions Proposed," para. 5.

8. On Christ as the agent in baptism, *Super Epistolam B. Pauli ad Ephesios lectura* 4.2 §200: "Baptisms do not differ by reason of who administers them. No matter who performs the rites they possess an unvaried power because he who baptizes interiorly is one, namely, Christ" (Thomas Aquinas, *Commentary on Saint Paul's Epistle to the Ephesians*, trans. Matthew Lamb [Albany, NY: Magi, 1966]). For a modern account of the sacraments influenced by Thomas, see A.-M. Roguet, *Christ Acts Through the Sacraments* (Collegeville, MN: Liturgical, 1954). Other theologians, while holding to the view that Christ as the chief minister of the sacraments, prefer to speak of the sacraments as exerting not instrumental but "moral" causality. For a discussion, see Joseph Pohle and Arthur Preuss, *The Sacraments* (St. Louis: Herder, 1942), 1:146–60.

other words, does the CDF's doctrinal note suggest that Thomas can be treated not merely as a theologian within the tradition, but as a question-settling authority? If this is the case, it is worrisome, since it takes Thomas out of the realm of theological argumentation and places him in the role of oracle, an oracle who has already answered all our questions and need only be consulted.

The Ebb and Flow of Thomas's Authority

Thomas was not always, of course, a figure of unquestioned oracular authority.[9] As Corey Barnes reminds us, "Before he became a received authority, Aquinas was a reader, teacher, and preacher amongst peers."[10] Indeed, he got off to a somewhat rocky start when, immediately after his death, some propositions drawn from his works were condemned by the bishop of Paris, and the Franciscans forbade their friars from reading his works without consulting a *correctorium* to steer them away from his errors. The general criticism was that Thomas was too wedded to Aristotle, too affirming of the integrity of nature, and too willing to let God's freedom be trapped by necessity. Many, though by no means all, of Thomas's fellow Dominicans came to his defense, and it was out of these early defenses that a "school" of Thomist thought was born. And though saintliness and theological acumen do not always go hand in hand, Thomas's reputation for genuine holiness helped ease his theological acceptance, and after his canonization in 1323 criticism was muted, if not absent.

Thomas accumulated authority slowly. Throughout the later Middle Ages, the Thomist school vied with Scotists, Albertists, Ockhamists, and others over a variety of theological and philosophical questions.[11] It is really in the sixteenth century, when the Protestant Reformation suggested

9. For the following paragraphs, see, among others, Romanus Cessario, *A Short History of Thomism* (Washington, DC: Catholic University of America Press, 2003), 40–81; Frederick J. Roensch, *Early Thomistic School* (Dubuque, IA: Priory, 1964). On the general topic of the role of Thomas in Catholic, Orthodox, and Protestant theology, see the compendious Matthew Levering and Marcus Plested, eds., *Oxford Handbook of the Reception of Aquinas* (Oxford: Oxford University Press, 2021).

10. Corey L. Barnes, "Thirteenth-Century Engagements with Thomas Aquinas," in Levering and Plested, *Oxford Handbook*, 33–34.

11. For a sense of the variety of scholastic schools in the later Middle Ages, see Ulrich G. Leinsle, *Introduction to Scholastic Theology*, trans. Michael J. Miller (Washington, DC: Catholic University of America Press, 2010), 182–242.

to Catholic leaders that the church needed to close ranks theologically, that Thomas began to emerge as the "common doctor." It may have helped Thomas's cause that Cajetan, who was one of the more able debaters of Lutherans, wrote a commentary on the *Summa theologiae*. Later, when the Jesuits emerged as key movers in the Catholic Reformation, the fact that St. Ignatius had made the *Summa theologiae* the staple of their theological education also helped solidify Thomas's reputation for reliable orthodoxy, and Jesuits like Robert Bellarmine made able use of Thomas in their controversial writings. And even if it is not true that a copy of the *Summa theologiae* lay on the altar beside the Bible at the Council of Trent, Thomas's influence on that council's teachings is undeniable, even as the door was left open—sometimes quite widely—for other schools of thought.

In the post-Tridentine era Thomas frequently appears to provide the proper answer to controverted questions. To choose a couple of examples from sacramental theology, we see the Holy Office of the Inquisition (the precursor to the CDF) take the Thomist side in the debate over whether the sacrament of penance could be conducted by mail, deciding no in 1602.[12] And in 1747, on the question of whether Jewish children could be baptized against the wishes of their parents, Benedict XIV invoked the authority of Thomas against the Scotists, again deciding no, and noting that "the opinion of St. Thomas prevailed in [canonical] courts . . . and is more widespread among theologians and those skilled in canon law" (D §2552–3). The notorious controversy *de auxiliis*, on grace and freedom, which ran through the seventeenth century and beyond, is noteworthy because it often seemed to be not a question whether Thomas's position was the correct one, but a question of exactly what Thomas's position was, with the implied corollary that Thomas's position, once discerned, would be correct. This was in part because the main controversialists, the Jesuits and the Dominicans, both claimed Thomas as their authoritative teacher.[13] The church, however, was scrupulous to avoid taking sides among what were considered a range of legitimate opinions. In some cases, most notably in the promotion and eventual definition of the doctrine of the immaculate conception, the church decided *against* Thomas's position. Still, even in these controverted cases, a

12. Heinrich Denzinger, *Compendium of Creeds, Definitions, and Declarations on Matter of Faith and Morals*, 43rd ed., ed. Peter Hünermann (San Francisco: Ignatius, 2012), §1994. Subsequently cited parenthetically as (D).

13. On the details of this controversy, see Matthew T. Gaetano, "The Catholic Reception of Aquinas in the *De Auxiliis* Controversy," in Levering and Plested, *Oxford Handbook*, 255–79.

nod is often given to Thomas as the norm of theological equanimity. Pope Benedict XIV wrote in 1753, "Since the Angelic Doctor is inscribed in the list of saints, although it may be permitted to think differently from him, nevertheless, it is not at all permitted to adopt a manner of acting and disputing different from his" (D §21671).

But it is really only in the mid-nineteenth century that Thomas achieves truly oracular status. We can see this at work in *Aeterni Patris*, the 1879 papal encyclical that did so much to establish Thomas as the norm of orthodoxy.[14] Pope Leo XIII presents Thomas as a figure uniquely capable of addressing all questions, past and future: "Single-handed, he victoriously combated the errors of former times, and supplied invincible arms to put those to rout which might in after-times spring up. . . . Reason, borne on the wings of Thomas to its human height, can scarcely rise higher, while faith could scarcely expect more or stronger aids from reason than those which she has already obtained through Thomas" (§18). Pope Leo presents Thomas, in Anselmian fashion, as that theologian than which no greater can be conceived. Leo allows that not all scholastic thought is suitable for the needs of the present day, writing, "If anything is taken up with too great subtlety by the Scholastic doctors, or too carelessly stated—if there be anything that ill agrees with the discoveries of a later age, or, in a word, improbable in whatever way—it does not enter Our mind to propose that for imitation to Our age" (§31). But he says this in the context of exhorting Catholic thinkers, "be ye watchful that the doctrine of Thomas be drawn from his own fountains, or at least from those rivulets which, derived from the very fount, have thus far flowed, according to the established agreement of learned men, pure and clear" (§31). Whatever flaws there may be in other scholastics, Thomas and his authentic interpreters seem to be free of them.

In other words, the thought of Thomas is evergreen and therefore stands ever ready to be pressed into service. And Thomas was pressed into service in the modernist crisis of the early twentieth century. In condemning modernism in the 1907 encyclical *Pascendi Dominici Gregis*,[15] Pius X wrote, "The passion for novelty is always united in them with hatred of scholasticism, and there is no surer sign that a man is on the way to

14. Leo XIII, *Aeterni Patris*, Vatican, August 4, 1879 (https://www.vatican.va/content/leo-xiii/en/encyclicals/documents/hf_l-xiii_enc_04081879_aeterni-patris.html). Cited parenthetically by paragraph number.

15. Pius X, *Pascendi Dominici Gregis*, Vatican, September 8, 1907 (https://www.vatican.va/content/pius-x/en/encyclicals/documents/hf_p-x_enc_19070908_pascendi-dominici-gregis.html). Cited parenthetically by paragraph number.

Modernism than when he begins to show his dislike for this system" (§42). He then goes on to clarify, "Let it be clearly understood above all things that the scholastic philosophy We prescribe is that which the Angelic Doctor [i.e., Thomas Aquinas] has bequeathed to us" (§45). I would note that here, as in *Aeterni Patris*, it is specifically the *philosophy* of Thomas that is commended as the foundation upon which all sound theology depends. But Pius's praise of Thomas grows ever more expansive, as philosophical authority bleeds into theological and even dogmatic authority. In a document directed a few years later to theological faculties in Italy, Pius wrote:

> The principles of philosophy laid down by St. Thomas Aquinas are to be religiously and inviolably observed, because they are the means of acquiring such a knowledge of creation as is most congruent with the Faith; of refuting all the errors of all the ages, and of enabling man to distinguish clearly what things are to be attributed to God and to God alone. . . . If Catholic doctrine is once deprived of this strong bulwark, it is useless to seek the slightest assistance for its defense in a philosophy whose principles are either common to the errors of materialism, monism, pantheism, socialism and modernism, or certainly not opposed to such systems. . . . If such principles are once removed or in any way impaired, it must necessarily follow that students of the sacred sciences will ultimately fail to perceive so much as the meaning of the words in which the dogmas of divine revelation are proposed by the magistracy of the Church.[16]

The twenty-four Thomist theses issued in July 1914 (D §§3601–3624) by the Vatican's Sacred Congregation of Studies, which were to provide norms for the philosophical formation of seminarians, seemed to come so close to simply identifying Catholic theology with Thomism that a subsequent clarification was issued, noting that these theses are proposed "as secure directional norms without, however, an obligation being imposed to accept all the theses."[17] A letter from Pope Benedict XV to the Superior General of the Jesuits, who feared that the twenty-four theses would forbid them to follow the views of their own tradition of scholastic interpretation, particularly that of Francisco Suarez, stated that the Roman pontiff's "constant opinion has been that St. Thomas should be considered the guide and teacher of studies in theology and philosophy, in which, however, anyone is free

16. Pius X, *Doctoris Angelici*, Jacques Maritain Center, June 29, 1914 (https://www3.nd.edu/~maritain/jmc/etext/doctoris.htm).

17. Congregation of Studies, March 7, 1916, *Acta Apostolica Sedes* 8, 157.

to dispute on either side about which one can and usually does dispute."[18] Apart from the question of what is included in the category of what "one can and usually does dispute," it is striking that it is precisely by the exceptional nature of the concessions to other theological schools that the normativity of Thomism is manifested. This normativity was manifested most clearly in the 1917 *Code of Canon Law*: "Professors shall treat studies in rational theology and philosophy and the instruction of students in these disciplines according to the system, teaching, and principles of the Angelic Doctor and hold to them religiously."[19] In this way, Thomas as a box of presorted philosophical answers quickly becomes Thomas as a source of theological doctrine, ready to hand for defeating the aberrations of modernity.

Of course, one cannot quite so easily put the modern genie back in the bottle, and the desire to critically appropriate modern thinking was not quenched by papal diktat. As Catholics engaged modern philosophical movements, the requirement of adhering to the thought of Thomas led to a proliferation of hyphenated Thomisms: transcendental-Thomism, existential-Thomism, phenomenogical-Thomism, and so forth. In some cases, these might have been disingenuous attempts at putting a Thomist fig leaf on modern philosophy, what the theologian Carlo Leget calls the "decorative" use of Thomas's authority,[20] but I tend to think that most were good-faith efforts to bring Thomas into conversation with modernity, rather than simply using him as a cudgel. If one reads in particular the early works of Karl Rahner or Bernard Lonergan, one sees a serious and rigorous engagement with Thomas, and even if in their later works there is not much explicit discussion of Thomas, they both remained clear on his continued importance.[21]

Yet Thomas did go into eclipse in Catholic theology after the Second Vatican Council. This was a result of the twin impulses at work at the Council: *ressourcement* or "returning to the sources," and *aggiornamento* or

18. Text cited in the introductory note to D §3601.

19. Canon 1366.

20. Carlo Leget, "Authority and Plausibility: Aquinas on Suicide," in Paul van Geest et al., eds., *Aquinas as Authority* (Leuven: Peeters, 2002), 277–93. Leget provides an extremely helpful taxonomy of different sorts of appeals to Thomas.

21. For Rahner, see *Spirit in the World*, trans. William V. Dych (New York: Herder and Herder, 1968), which originally appeared in German in 1939. For Longergan, see *Verbum: Word and Idea in Aquinas*, ed. Frederick Crowe and Robert Doran (Toronto: University of Toronto Press, 1997), originally published between 1946 and 1949 as a series of five articles in the journal *Theological Studies*.

"updating." Advocates of *ressourcement* sought to overcome a sclerotic neo-scholasticism and renew theology by returning to the sources of theology: Scripture, the liturgy, and the church fathers. While in most cases careful not to explicitly reject Thomas, these *ressourcement* theologians relativized his importance by turning to patristic sources, particularly Augustine and the Greek fathers, in whom, the argument went, theology and spirituality had not yet undergone the separation they would suffer at the hands of scholasticism's efforts to make theology "scientific." Thomas was often honored as an exemplary medieval instance of how the sources of theology might be engaged, but in no sense as a replacement for our own engagement with those sources.[22] Advocates of *aggiornamento*, on the other hand, tended to simply replace Thomas as a foundation for theology with modern philosophy, critical history, and the social sciences, often unironically appealing to the authority of Thomas for doing so: just as Thomas replaced Platonism with the more "up-to-date" Aristotelian philosophy of his day, so too we should replace Thomism with Heideggerian phenomenology, or critical reconstructions of the historical Jesus, or Marxist social analysis. Thomas was engaged not so much as a theological interlocutor, much less a theological oracle, but as an authority for keeping theology abreast of the latest intellectual trends. This view was expressed recently by the historian Massimo Faggioli, who speaks of the recognition by what he calls "'progressive' neo-Thomists" (which to some might seem like a contradiction in terms) of the need "to adopt Thomas's approach rather than his conclusions."[23] The net result of both of these movements was what Karl Rahner called a "strange silence on the subject of Thomas Aquinas" among theologians after the council.[24] I recall a Dominican who went through formation in the 1980s telling me that, though they of course studied St. Thomas in their philosophy classes, in theology classes the Dominican

---

22. This paints the picture of *ressourcement* theology with far too broad a brush, of course. Many *ressourcement* theologians—not only Dominicans like Marie-Dominique Chenu, but also Jesuits like Henri de Lubac—were extremely robust in engaging Thomas's thought. For a sense of the variety of approaches that might be gathered under the *ressourcement* umbrella, see the essays in Gabriel Flynn and Paul Murray, eds., *Ressourcement: A Movement for Renewal in Twentieth-Century Catholic Theology* (Oxford: Oxford University Press, 2012).

23. Massimo Faggioli, *Vatican II: The Battle for Meaning* (New York: Paulist, 2012), 79.

24. Karl Rahner, *Theological Investigations*, trans. D. Bourke (New York: Seabury, 1975), 13:3.

theologian they were likely to read was Edward Schillebeeckx rather than Thomas.

But, as happens so often in the ebb and flow of theological fortune, Thomas has recently made something of a comeback. This is true not only among Dominicans, where it might be expected, but also among younger lay theologians. I can only speculate as to the reasons for this. Thomas is still a figure to be reckoned with who, particularly among nonspecialists in medieval theology, is in some ways the most accessible representative of the scholastic tradition. He is an extraordinarily good theologian, and, once you master the format of a scholastic article and the basics of his vocabulary, he is actually pretty easy to read. Plus, all of his works are readily available on the internet, most of them in translation. Perhaps most of all, for younger theologians seeking refuge from what some see as the decades of theological chaos following the Second Vatican Council, Thomas seems to be a ready port of refuge. The *Summa theologiae* itself can seem like a great big book of answers to just about any theological question. And, as in years past, it is easy to get the impression that to locate yourself on the side of Thomas is to locate yourself on the side of the church. This is not by any means to denigrate recent work employing Thomas, much of which is of extraordinarily high quality, but simply to account for its prevalence. And if I am right in my speculation—even, perhaps, only partly right—then we might be justified in worrying that Thomas might end up being turned back into an oracle rather than a (particularly good) theologian with whom we are invited to engage.

We-Baptism Revisited

How then ought we to engage Thomas theologically? To suggest how this might be done, I would like to return to the question of the baptismal formula and its validity. Thomas, of course, is not the only theologian in the tradition who addressed the question of what sort of variations might be admitted in the words of baptism without compromising the validity of the sacrament. Much medieval discussion of the sacramental sign of baptism concerned the various ways in which one could screw up the name of the Trinity. The most famous case can be found in a letter written in the eighth century by St. Boniface to Pope Zachary. Boniface discovered that a parish priest had been baptizing with the words *Baptizo te in nomine patria et filia et spiritus sancti* (I baptize you in the name of the Fatherland, and of the daughter, and of the Holy Spirit), so he asked the pope whether these baptisms should be held to be invalid. The pope replied that since the man acted out of ignorance, and the change of endings did not entirely obscure the meaning, the baptisms should be considered valid.[25] Pope Alexander III in the twelfth century addressed the importance of saying "I baptize you"— in contrast not with saying "*we* baptize" but rather with saying nothing at all—i.e., simply pouring water while saying "in the name of the Father" etc. It seems that what is significant for Alexander is not so much the pronoun as the verb, in order to distinguish the baptismal washing from other rituals one might enact with water.[26] Thomas's contemporary Bonaventure addressed the possibility that one might interrupt the Trinitarian formula, perhaps by sneezing or by interjecting a comment such as "hmmm, this water is cold" (*aqua ista est frigida*), and concluded that a short interruption would not invalidate the baptism, though if one were to preach a homily between the naming of the Father and the naming of the Son, or leave to urinate between the naming of the Son and the naming of the Holy Spirit, then one should really start the baptismal formula over again.[27]

But to my knowledge (which, to be sure, is nowhere near comprehensive), Thomas is unique in addressing the question of the we-formula, which perhaps justifies the CDF turning to him for a clear answer. But is the answer really so clear? It is worth spelling out the argument as we find it in Thomas himself. The point at issue in the text cited by the CDF (*ST* 3.67.6) is not simply whether one can use "we" instead of "I," but whether several ministers could perform one baptism together. First, Thomas asks, what if they did so by division of labor, with one pouring the water and the other saying the formula, an occasion that might arise, he notes in an earlier article, if one minister were mute and the other lacked hands (see *ST* 3.66.5 ad 4)? Thomas says that this would be invalid because it would decompose the sacramental sign, which consists of both form (the words) and matter (the washing with water). But what if both ministers were to perform the sacramental sign—form and matter—simultaneously? Then, Thomas asks, what formula would they use? It is in this context that he disallows the we-formula, since it reflects a mode of baptism that seems to deny that the baptizer acts ministerially in the place of Christ (since Christ is an "I" and not a "we"). Thomas then envisions two baptizers both using the "I" formula, in

25. Letter LIV, Zacharias to Boniface (July 1, 746), D §588.

26. Gregory IX, *Decretals* 3, t. 42, c. 1.

27. *In Sent.* 5 d. 3 p. 1 a. 2 q. 3 ad 5.

which case the person *would* be validly baptized, though only by whichever minister gets to the end of the baptismal formula first, which would make the slower minister liable for the crime of attempting to rebaptize someone. And if they managed to speak the formula with absolute simultaneity, while they would be guilty of baptizing in an improper way, Thomas tells us that "the one Christ baptizing inwardly would confer one sacrament by means of both together." So Thomas's main concern in this particular article seems to be with splitting the baptismal sign between two ministers,[28] and it is in this context that Thomas presents the we-formula as problematic. Thomas says clearly, "As there is one Christ, so there should only be one minister who represents Christ," and he disallows the we-formula as a way around having a single minister.

But does the we-formula used by a single minister—as in the two contemporary cases with which I began—present the same problem? This is a question Thomas does not address. Despite the use of the pronoun "we," there is still a single person acting ministerially *in persona Christi*, just as there is a single person acting ministerially in the sacrifice of the Mass, even though the Roman Canon says "we make humble prayer and petition" and "we offer you this sacrifice of praise" and "we celebrate the memorial of the blessed Passion" and "we, your servants and your holy people, offer . . . this spotless victim." Indeed, in none of the eucharistic prayers currently authorized in the Roman Rite does the celebrant speak in the first-person singular (except when the bishop celebrates Mass and prays for himself as "me, your unworthy servant"), and yet no one sees this as undermining the teaching that it is the priest alone who acts ministerially.[29]

---

28. And lest you think this is an improbable scenario, a friend of mine recently served as godfather at a conditional rebaptism that was occasioned when an adult discovered a photo of her baptism as an infant where it appeared that her original godfather was pouring the water while the priest recited the baptismal formula. I myself have seen occasions of the baptismal formula being divided among three ministers—one for each person of the Trinity—which raises not only questions of sacramental theology, but also the specter of tritheism. So Thomas's concern for the possible mutilation of the sacramental sign is not simply the product of a fevered scholastic imagination.

29. Of course, Thomas has to reckon with the fact that the Roman Rite, in the practice of concelebration, actually allows more than one priest to act ministerially in the eucharistic consecration and sacrifice. Though the practice was rarer in Thomas's day than it is today—being restricted to the ordination Mass of a priest—he does address the question of whether more than one priest could consecrate the same host. Thomas says yes, arguing "the priest does not consecrate except *in persona Christi*; and since many are one in Christ (Gal 3:28); consequently it does not matter whether this sacrament be consecrated by one or by many" (*ST* 3.82.2). Thomas is aware this seems to contradict what he said

In the case of the eucharistic prayer, the use of the first-person plural need not be a denial that the one speaking is acting ministerially in the name of Christ, and by analogy this suggests that the we-formula in baptism need not constitute such a denial either. To use the terminology of speech-act theory, we need to attend not simply to the illocutionary act, but to the perlocutionary effects of the sacramental sign—that is to say not simply the dictionary meaning of the words as spoken, but the total effect of the speech-act in its concrete circumstances of utterance. Indeed, if we think of the complex of signs in which the words of baptism are embedded, it seems unlikely that those witnessing the event would think that anyone other than the minister who spoke the words and poured the water had performed the baptism. If someone asked, "Who baptized Sally?" it would be only someone with a particular theological agenda who would answer, "We all did," and such a person would likely give this answer no matter whether the minister said "we" or "I." Given the context, anyone else would answer, "Father McGillicuddy."

Perhaps we might think about Thomas's own arguments as speech acts, possessed of a perlocutionary effect that is shaped by the context of the illocutionary act. Or to put it more simply, for Thomas, as for any theologian, context matters, and perhaps we should not presume that Thomas has "already" asked and answered precisely the question we are asking today. One of the dangers of turning a theologian into an oracle is that his or her utterances become decontextualized. The CDF decontextualizes Thomas's statement about the we-formula, and if we recontextualize it—for example, locate it within a discussion of multiple ministers attempting to baptize someone—we might find a bit more wiggle room in our own grappling with the questions that arise in our own context.

But the context of Thomas's statements about the we-formula of baptism is not simply the larger argument within which he makes it. Thomas's context also includes the world of thirteenth-century theology and what was and wasn't known at the time, particularly about the historical variations in Christian practice concerning the baptismal formula. Some of this variation Thomas *was* aware of. Like other medieval theologians, he knew that the book of Acts spoke of baptism "in the name of Jesus Christ" (8:12) and, as the article of the *Summa* that discusses this question shows,

---

earlier with regard to baptism, but his response to the seeming contradiction—"We do not read of Christ baptizing with the apostles when he committed to them the duty of baptizing; consequently there is no parallel"—is not entirely satisfying.

he was aware that there was a diversity of views on whether such a thing could constitute true baptism, with Ambrose and Pope Nicholas I saying it could and Pope Pelagius II and Didymus saying it could not. Thomas at first seems to take the harder line, writing, "If any of those things are omitted that Christ instituted concerning a sacrament, it loses its efficacy"; but he then adds a qualifying clause, "unless by special dispensation of him who did not bind his power to the sacraments" (*ST* 3.66.6). He sees the baptisms in Acts as valid, therefore, because God gave precisely such a dispensation, "in order that the name of Christ, which was odious to Jews and Gentiles, might be rendered honorable" (*ST* 3.66.6 ad 1).

Thomas was also aware that in the Greek churches baptisms are performed in the passive voice: "The servant of God, N., is baptized in the name of the Father, and of the Son, and of the Holy Spirit"—circumventing the I-we question entirely. Thomas notes that the omission of any reference to who is baptizing is done for the sake of combatting the view that ascribes the efficacy of baptism to the minister, which he sees reflected in 1 Cor 1:12: "I am of Paul . . . and I of Cephas." While he thinks the Latin form more clearly expresses the intention, the Greek form is allowable, not simply by divine dispensation (as in the case of baptism in the name of Christ) but by being the ordinary practice of the church. What is essential is the triune name: "Since the action performed by the minister is expressed with the invocation of the Trinity, the sacrament is truly accomplished" (*ST* 3.66.5 ad 1).[30] Why then is the case different for the we-formula? We can only speculate, but perhaps Thomas would argue that, whereas the Greek formula simply leaves the agent unspecified, the we-formula seems to contradict what the Latin formula says—that it is the singular *I*, acting in the name of Christ, that is performing this baptism. Or, perhaps less speculatively, it may be simply that the Greek formula is a long-standing and widespread practice of half of Christendom, and Thomas's basic principle in sacramental theology (though he never puts it this way) is *lex orandi stat lex credendi*—the law of prayer establishes the law of believing.

But what about other rules of prayer of which Thomas was unaware? What, for example, of the rite of baptism described in the so-called *Apostolic Tradition*, from the third century, which seems to lack any baptismal formula whatsoever, having instead an immersion after each response of "I believe" by the one being baptized to the credal questions "Do you believe in God the Father Almighty? . . . Do you believe in Christ Jesus, the son

30. Cf. Aquinas, *Super I Epistolam B. Pauli ad Corinthios lectura* cap. 1 lec. 2 §25.

of God? . . . Do you believe in the Holy Spirit?"[31] And, lest we think this simply some odd one-off in the early liturgical tradition, this mode of baptism by interrogation seems also to be witnessed to by St. Ambrose in the late fourth century.[32] Nor was this a Milanese peculiarity, since Ambrose tells us that, with the exception of Milan's practice of washing the feet of the newly baptized, regarding the church of Rome, "her type and form we follow in all things."[33] Had Thomas known this, would he have allowed for this on the basis of its antiquity and the authority of Ambrose, despite Pope Alexander's insistence on the inclusion of the word "baptize" among the words used in baptizing?

What, then, of the form used in the baptism of one Probus, recounted in the mid-third-century *Acts of Xanthippe and Polyxena*, which says—you guessed it—"We baptize you . . ."?[34] If Thomas had been aware of this ancient practice, would it have pressed him to consider the case of a single minister using the "we" formula, and if he had considered it, would he have found a way to allow for it, as he had for the Greek formula? My own sense of Thomas is that, given the importance of actual liturgical practice to his thinking about the sacraments, he might have, but that is of course simply speculation on my part. He might very well have concluded that poor Probus was not validly baptized and should be baptized again *in forma absoluta*. We simply do not know.

What we do know is that the scholastic revolution of the twelfth and thirteenth centuries was based on an awareness of conflicts within the tradition and on the use of reason to adjudicate those conflicts. So for a scholastic like Thomas the existence of a plurality of Christian practices with regard to baptism was not an insurmountable problem, but simply an invitation to think through the conflicts this plurality generated. In this particular case, perhaps Massimo Faggioli is correct that we should follow Thomas's approach rather than his conclusions. Thomas and the other medieval scholastics should be for us models, not oracles, because we know things that they could not know, and we ask questions that they

---

31. Hippolytus, *Apostolic Tradition* 21:12–18 (*On the Apostolic Tradition*, ed. and trans. Alistair Stewart-Sykes [Crestwood, NY: St. Vladimir's Seminary Press, 2001]).

32. Ambrose, *De sacramentis* 2.7.20 (*St. Ambrose on the Sacraments and on the Mysteries*, ed. J. H. Srawley, trans. T. Thompson [London: SPCK, 1950]).

33. Ambrose, *De sacramentis* 3.1.5.

34. In E. C. Witaker, *Documents of the Baptismal Liturgy*, 2nd ed. (London: SPCK, 1970), 20.

did not ask.[35] In the case of the formula "we baptize, " it is natural to turn to Thomas, since we don't have much else in the tradition to turn to with this question, and Thomas does seem to address it. But the brief discussion from Thomas cited by the CDF addresses a situation that is not precisely identical to the modern situation. Moreover, it is an argument that does not consider all of the evidence that we have today regarding the variability of the baptismal formula in history.

All of which is to say that the CDF could have decided differently, despite the authority of Thomas. After all, the church has in the recent past disagreed with Thomas on sacramental questions, such as the proper form and matter of Holy Orders, though it rarely points out that it is disagreeing with him.[36] At the very least, taking into account what we know today about the diversity of ancient baptismal practice, an element of uncertainty might have led to practical recommendations for remedying any defect in baptisms performed with the we-formula that were different than what seems to me the rather drastic act of a baptism *in forma absoluta*.[37] My fear is that

35. This is above all the case in practical questions. Contrary to the implicit claims of some forms of liberal Christianity, we do not acquire new data about the great mysteries of faith—I don't think we could unearth a manuscript that would lead us to rethink the Holy Trinity or the incarnation—but about how the mysteries of faith might be enacted in practice.

36. On the form and matter of sacrament of Orders, compare Thomas—"The matter of this sacrament is that matter which is handed over to the candidate at the conferring of the order. Thus, priesthood is conferred by the handing over of the chalice, and so each order is conferred by the handing over of that matter which in a special way pertains to the ministry of that particular order. The form of this sacrament is this: 'receive the power to offer sacrifice in the church for the living and the dead'" (*On the Articles of Faith and the Sacraments of the Church* 2.7)—and Pius XII, *Sacramentum Ordinis* (1947)—"the matter, and the only matter, of the Sacred Orders of the Diaconate, the Priesthood, and the Episcopacy is the imposition of hands; and . . . the form, and the only form, is the words which determine the application of this matter, which univocally signify the sacramental effects" (§4).

37. One obvious alternative pastoral solution would be to recommend conditional baptism rather than baptism *in forma absoluta*. Another, less obvious solution might be modeled on marriages that are deemed invalid due to lack of canonical form—i.e., one or both of them being Catholic, a couple chooses to wed in a non-Catholic marriage ceremony, and without obtaining a dispensation to do so. The church deems such marriages putatively invalid on the presumption that the Catholic party or parties chose to marry outside the church because they did not intend to enter into what the church considers a valid marriage—i.e., they had a defective intention. Such cases are normally resolved via convalidation, in which the couple speak their vows before a Catholic minister. This presumes that up to that point the couple was not validly married, and in this way it is analogous to remedying a defective baptism via baptism *in forma absoluta*. An

the belief that, as the CDF doctrinal note puts it, "Thomas Aquinas had already asked himself the question" gives a sense of false confidence where a somewhat more cautious approach might be called for, particularly when the pastoral fallout of such a decision might well spread far and wide.

The thought of Thomas Aquinas is a great blessing to the church. But that blessing remains a blessing only so long as we do not treat Thomas's thought as identical to the mind of the church. Thomas devoted his life to thinking about the mystery of God, and never mistook his own thoughts for the reality of that mystery. What Thomas says about other doctors of the church should apply to the Angelic Doctor as well: "The authority of other church teachers [*doctorum ecclesiae*] may properly be used in arguing, though only as probable. For our faith rests upon the revelation made to the apostles and prophets who wrote the canonical books, and not on the revelations—if there are any—made to other teachers" (*ST* 1.1.8). As Thomas reminded the world at the end of his life, his words were not divine oracles, but straw upon which the sparks of the Spirit might fall. We would do well to keep this in mind.

---

alternative solution is what is known as "radical sanation" (i.e., "healing at the root"), in which an investigation is carried out to determine whether or not the couple's intention at the time of the marriage was defective. If it is discovered that it was not defective—i.e., if they intended to do what the church intends by marriage—then their marriage is deemed valid and no repetition of vows is required. Perhaps cases of baptism according to the we-formula could be handled in a similar way: an investigation could be carried out to determine whether the minister who performed the baptism, despite using the we-formula, intended to act as the sole ministerial representative of Christ and simply did not understand how the word "we" might be contradictory to that intention. If this were found to be the case, then the original baptism would be, as it were, healed at the root, and there would be no need for a new baptism, whether *in forma absoluta* or conditionally.

Rite Issues, Wrong Answers: Luther and the Canon of the Mass

By Amy C. Schifrin

WHEN I WAS FIRST asked about presenting a paper on the topic of what one of our favorite theologians, Martin Luther, got "wrong," I compiled a list. As one whose family members were slaughtered in the pogroms of Odessa, shot wholesale and buried in the ditches of Belarus, and treated worse than farm animals in the extermination camps of Poland until their bodies were turned to dust, Luther's little tract *On the Jews and Their Lies* was the first thing that came to my mind. He may have said nice things in the past. He may have been suffering from uremic poisoning. Certainly he was dealing with kidney stones, which could make anyone sound nasty, and unquestionably he was a man of his times. But truth be told, he was far less an anti-Jew than that great anti-Semite Ulrich Zwingli, who even forbade singing and chanting in his churches because he didn't want these good Christian people "murmuring like the Jews."[1]

Then I thought about Luther's tract *Against the Murderous and Thieving Hordes of Peasants*. I thought about the beautiful and extremely hardworking folks among whom I worked in El Salvador, Guatemala, El Paso, and Ciudad Juarez. Even if his biting invective was due to some health problem, even if the peasants had missed his intentions when he wrote of Christian freedom, his words gave permission to the landowners "to strike down the peasants like one would do with a mad dog."[2] One hundred thou-

1. Paul Westermeyer, *Te Deum: The Church and Music* (Minneapolis: Fortress, 1998), 151.

2. Martin Luther, *Against the Thieving and Murdering Hoards of Peasants*, in Theodore

sand of God's children were slaughtered. And his writings were used to fuel a particular brand of quietism, one which allowed those in civil authority to retain power, even if that authority was harvested off the backs of serfs and slaves, who were seen as commodities to be exploited and treated as expendable. Centuries later, this alignment with those who held temporal power was interpreted in the worst possible way, as when the Reich Kirche was formed in 1934. While he would not have known of the death count to come from that unholy alliance, I still count *Against the Murderous and Thieving Hordes of Peasants* among Luther's greatest errors.

Of course, there were also a few other odd and unusual biblical interpretations. I mean, what was he thinking about when he read the Song of Solomon? When you hear, "O that you would kiss me with the kisses of your mouth! For your love is better than wine," do you think "encomium of the political order"? (We really should ask Katie about that. [Katie was Luther's wife.]) Yet, this may somehow relate to his framing of the 1529 *Order of Marriage for Common Pastors*, which moves the wedding rite closer to the civil rather than the sacramental realm (i.e., no nuptial Mass).[3] And thus, looking at rites, which are all interconnected in a ritual system, we are brought to what I have experienced as one of the most neuralgic of issues among North American Lutherans, long fought among the brothers and sisters with the toxicity of one suffering from uremic poisoning, as well as an invective that sounds like it comes straight from the gates of hell. The issue is about ritual, most pointedly about the eucharistic rites through which the gathered assembly receives the gifts of the Risen Christ. Whatever we call it, it is at the heart of our life of faith: the Sacrament of the Altar, Holy Communion, Eucharist, the Divine Service, *Gottesdienst*, the Mass—and Luther wants us to know he did not abolish the Mass.[4] Born out of interpretations and disputes that grew from the fourth century all the way into the High Middle Ages, Luther takes his turn as he seeks to right what had gone wrong with the rite, especially a deficient sacramentalism, which he saw took away the gifts of God from the people of God. Among his major concerns, which were framed through his understanding of justification by faith, were that the Mass was now considered to be both a work, i.e., not a religious or pious work but an attempt to attain something from God,

---

G. Tappert, ed., *Selected Writings of Martin Luther* (Philadelphia: Fortress, 1967), 186–94.

3. Martin Luther, *Liturgy and Hymns*, ed. Ulrich S. Leupold (Philadelphia: Fortress, 1965), 110.

4. Luther, *Liturgy and Hymns*, 20; see also art. 24 of the Augsburg Confession.

but without faith,[5] and second, a sacrifice, something that diminished the salvific work and the person of Jesus Christ. *Opus bonum et sacrificium*: these acts would fall under the rubrics of works-righteousness and idolatry. As Luther writes,

> It is Christ's intention . . . that the sacrament be dispensed to Christ's congregation, in order to strengthen its faith and to praise God publicly; but you have made a work of your own out of it, which is supposed to be yours and which you have accomplished without the assistance of any other person and such work you have dispensed to others and sold for money.[6]

Luther was not opposed to referring the bread and wine and any other gifts collected at the offering as either sacrifice or oblations if they weren't being offered for special intentions, but once consecrated they should be received only by the assembly as gifts. The church has no power to offer them to God.

Some late twentieth- and early twenty-first-century Lutherans have not concerned themselves with questions about the Eucharist and eucharistic praying. They have accepted, generally without question, Luther's recension of the Roman Canon in his *Formula missae et communiones* of 1523, and even more so, his further pruning of the text (and actions) of the Mass in his *Deutsche Messe*, a folk Mass of 1526, as now serving as the final word for the template of "Lutheran" liturgy for all time. Yet, Luther himself said not to do so. As Luther wrote, "In the first place, I would kindly and for God's sake request all those who see this order of service and desire to follow it: Do not make it a rigid law to bind or entangle anyone's conscience but use it in Christian liberty as long, when, where, and how you find it to be practical and useful."[7] (But once you provide a simple order, like a slip-

---

5. As opposed to a "work" in a cultic sense: "Now when Luther maintained that the mass had been made into a 'work' he does not mean by this word simply an external, ritual action. His contention takes into account the religiously serious striving which aims to attain something from God, but without faith. The mass as opus is not simply a superstition, it is primarily legalism. With the term 'work' reference is made quite inclusively to a spiritual attitude which does not stand face to face with God purely and simply to receive, but wants to present piety to him." Carl L. Wisloff, *The Gift of Communion*, quoted in Frank C. Senn, *Christian Liturgy: Catholic and Evangelical* (Minneapolis: Fortress, 1997), 270. See also Senn, "Towards a Different Anaphoral Structure," *Worship* 5 (July 1984) 358.

6. Martin Luther, *D. Martin Luthers Werke: Kritische Gesamtausgabe* (Weimar: Böhlau, 1883–2009), 38:199.

7. Luther, *Liturgy and Hymns*, 20.

pery cat let out of the bag, there's no easy way to put it back in without a lots of hissing and biting.)

Yet I, on the other hand, struggled to make sense of this utilitarian minimalism in what I, now one among the baptized, had come to believe was the pinnacle of the Catholic and evangelical liturgy, a full Trinitarian eucharistic prayer in which God the Father is blessed and thanked, salvation history is polysemously and doxologically prayed and proclaimed, the Holy Spirit is petitioned to make our hearts new, and all the baptized receive the body and blood of Christ so that we might live as God intended for us to live as *homo adorans*, the worshipping human. God gives himself to us, his body into ours, so that we would live out his goodness, his kindness, his mercy, his forgivingness, in hopes that people of every tribe and nation would receive and rejoice in his gift of eternal love. The liturgy of the Eucharist, from invocation to benediction, is a performative doxological eucharistic exegesis of the One who is the ever-living Word.[8] God is present at all times, but within the sacred frame of ritual he makes his mercy known with particularity, for it is in the way that he has promised to be with us. For having grown up in the land of *tallises* and Torah, in a conservative, leaning-toward-Orthodox, Ashkenazi shul, where the wailing of the shofar called me to live a holy life, where we sang and danced, and where little ones were twirled high in the air in a manner of ecstatic joy, this new-to-me Lutheran eucharistic minimalism (*verba* only) seemed to be devoid of life. It seemed like folks really didn't believe that anything of true importance was happening when they gathered for "worship."

Event had been flattened into text, and saying the right words was all that mattered. But the synagogue had been the place where I learned that if you could chant something important once, you wouldn't just want to chant it a couple of times, you'd want to chant it far too many times to count, until it was embedded in every fiber of your being, so that not only did you carry it in your heart, God carried you through each note in his. *Shema Yisroel Adonai Elohenu Adonai Ehud.* So, I could not understand why people who were baptized in the name of the Father and of the Son and of the Holy Spirit, people whose identity was given to them as water was poured and the word spoken, why such people wouldn't want a full Trinitarian eucharistic prayer when they came together to be strengthened

---

8. With this phrase I am expanding on the thought of Richard Lischer as he speaks in regard to the sermon, "A biblical sermon is an exposition of the Scripture, which is an exposition of the gospel, which is an exposition of the life of God." Richard Lischer, *A Theology of Preaching: The Dynamics of the Gospel* (Eugene, OR: Wipf & Stock, 1992), 59.

and renewed for all that lay ahead in this hurting world. For just as in the chanting of the Shema, so, now, from the invocation to the creed to the eucharistic acclamation—*Christ has died. Christ is risen. Christ will come again*—our identities as beloved of God were being shaped and deepened to live out our lives in great thanksgiving.

So, why did Luther prune supplications of the canon of the *Missa Romanum*? Why did he remove all the non-biblical words? Why did he focus on the words of institution as all that was needed to consecrate the elements? Why no epiclesis? Why no distinct Trinitarian structure? Why move the Sanctus yet retain the elevation? Where did all of this liturgical "adaptation" come from? How, through both words and actions, could Luther shape the Mass so that it was evident to the people that the consecration was the work of God, by the word of Christ, rather than by the power of the priest? It was much to my surprise when I began to explore this question a "few" decades ago, for along the way I learned that much of what Luther had done to shape his 1523 *Missa Formulae* (and that reshaping was basically limited to the canon of the Mass not to the full liturgical order), was in some way the logical conclusion of a movement that began to go astray as far back as the fourth century.[9] He wasn't the first one to have the rite issues, but the wrong answers.

Ambrose of Milan emphasized the words of institution as that which was consecratory (*verba consecrationes*),[10] rather than the whole eucharistic prayer, although not all of the earliest known manuscripts of Eucharist prayers, such as Addai and Mari or the Didache, contained the words of institution.[11] Ambrose may not have known of the epicletic tradition of which Cyril of Jerusalem wrote in his *Mystagogical Catecheses* in which God was implored "to send forth his Holy Spirit upon the offering to make the bread the body of Christ and the wine the blood of Christ."[12] In John Chrysostom's eucharistic praying there is both an institution narrative and an epiclesis, and it is the Holy Spirit who is called up to make the change

9. Frank C. Senn, "Martin Luther's Revision of the Eucharistic Canon in the Formula Missae of 1523," *Currents in Theology and Mission* 44 (1973) 101–18, esp. 106.

10. Ambrose, *De mysteriis* 9 and *De sacramentis* 4, quoted in Senn, "Martin Luther's Revision," 106, 108.

11. R. C. D. Jasper and G. J. Cuming, *Prayers of the Eucharist: Early and Reformed*, 4th ed. (Collegeville, MN: Liturgical, 2019), 39, 64.

12. A. Hanggi and I. Paul, *Prex Eucharistica*, quoted in Senn, *Christian Liturgy*, 243. See also Anne McGowan, *Eucharistic Epiclesis Ancient and Modern: Speaking of the Spirit in Eucharistic Prayer* (Collegeville, MN: Liturgical, 2014), 35–39.

of the elements into the body and blood of our Lord. Yet in his writing Chrysostom refers to both the institution and epiclesis in transforming the gifts, because what lies behind this are Christ's words, which are "eternally efficacious."[13] Although not all the earliest prayers contain an epiclesis, there is an epicletic or petitionary cast to the eucharistic texts indicating that the presence of God is not accomplished by the priest's power, but by the will of God, whose promises are trustworthy. Theodore of Mopsuestia was not alone among the fathers to liken the work of the Holy Spirit at the Eucharist to the incarnational work of the Holy Spirit in Mary's womb. This could be thought of as a parallel type of work bringing about the presence of Christ.

So it was from Ambrose that the church heard,

> For the sacrament which you receive, is effected by the words of Christ. . . . The Lord Jesus himself declares: "This is my body." Before the benediction of the heavenly words another species is mentioned; after the consecration the body is signified. He himself speaks of his blood. Before the consecration it is mentioned as something else; after the consecration it is called blood.[14]

Although it is not easy to tell if Augustine, some years later, is speaking of the eternally efficacious word of Christ or the words of celebrant, he did fall in line with Ambrose in that the speaking of the *verba* was the moment of consecration. This trajectory continued through the Middle Ages and took on a precise focus in Aquinas, for in a comparison analogous to what is necessary for a valid baptism, even if everything but the *verba* was omitted from the canon of the Mass, Aquinas wrote that the sacrament would still be valid, although a sin against the church would have been committed.[15]

In those intervening centuries the emphasis on the real presence of Christ grew amid controversies. Proscriptions involving the manual acts

---

13. Senn reminds of Atchley's proposal "that in Chrysostom's view the words of Christ, spoken once, are eternally efficacious, so that in the last analysis it is Christ who consecrates the bread and wine. As Christ's minister, the priest speaks the words of Christ but it is God who gives them their power through the invocation of the Holy Spirit." E. G. Cuthbert F. Atchley, *On the Epiclesis of the Eucharistic Liturgy and in the Consecration of the Font*, quoted in Senn, *Christian Liturgy*, 244.

14. Ambrose, *De mysteriis* 9.52–54, quoted in Senn, *Christian Liturgy*, 245.

15. Senn, "Martin Luther's Revision," 107.

emerged.[16] The meaning of priestly ordination was honed,[17] for as the ordinands were handed (*traditio instrumentorum*) the chalice and paten, the bishop would proclaim, "Receive the power of offering sacrifice for the living and the dead."[18] The dogma of transubstantiation also played into defining the Eucharist as the "Sacrifice of the Mass."[19] Ocular communion/ veneration of the consecrated elements replaced actually physically receiving the sacrament. The doctrine of the real presence combined with the West's earlier move way back in the third century from the term *eucharistia* to *oblatio* and *sacrificium* led to an understanding that the sacrifice had already begun with the offertory. So here, Luther, again, is headed to the right questions.

As fewer and fewer of the laity were actually communing, the nature of the offertory changed. From the third century on, when the offertory took on greater significance as the importance of the goodness of God's creation was being attacked by the Gnostics, bread and wine were not just brought forth from the assembly, they were offered to God.[20] But in the ensuing centuries, large quantities of bread and wine were no longer needed for the Mass as fewer and fewer lay people were receiving. They were taught that they were unworthy, and not being schooled in Latin, they could only see the gestures of the priest but were without hearing or understanding of the words. This happened in the same time frame as the growth of the

16. John F. Baldovin, "Accepit Panem: The Gestures of the Priest at the Institution Narrative of the Eucharist," in Nathan Mitchell and John F. Baldovin, eds., *Rule of Prayer, Rule of Faith: Essays in Honor of Aidan Kavanagh, OSB* (Collegeville, MN: Liturgical, 1996), 123–29.

17. "What can get veiled by a narrow use of the *in persona Christi* axiom is the fact that the primary ritual agent in the celebration of the Eucharist is not God, nor even the priest celebrant, but the assembly." (I would nuance this to say it is both God and the assembly, and the assembly includes the priest.) Daly reminds us of what happens when the priest acting *in persona Christi*, loses the second half of the phrase, *Christi capitis ecclesiae*. Robert J. Daly, *Sacrifice Unveiled: The True Meaning of Christian Sacrifice* (London: T&T Clark, 2009), 144.

18. "In Catholic thinking (that survives in popular forms even to this day), it was assumed that the priest received in ordination the personal power to carry out the Eucharistic sacrifice. This was thought of more as a personal, proprietary power adhering to his individual person rather than a mandate or a commission to lead the assembly in celebrating the Eucharist." Daly, *Sacrifice Unveiled*, 146.

19. Bard Thompson, *Liturgies of the Western Church* (Cleveland: Meridian, 1962), 42–43.

20. Joseph Jungmann, *The Early Liturgy* (South Bend, IN: University of Notre Dame Press, 1965), 116.

practice of priests receiving stipends "to offer the sacrifice of the mass for special intentions to benefit the living and the dead."[21] Although the *Ordo Roman Primus* called for all the gifts to be elevated, now just the host and chalice were elevated. As this was experienced in combination with the priests receiving a stipend for the Mass for special intentions, what was now commonly understood was that the bread and wine had been changed into the body and blood of Christ to be offered on behalf of those who had paid the Mass stipend, the "special intention for the benefit of the living and the dead."[22]

Instead of having faith in the one God who breathed life into all things, faith was misplaced in the one who had the power to confect the sacrament, and who then could offer this confected sacrament on behalf of those whose coins were lining the church's pockets. Rather than trusting in the One whose sacrifice of love was for all times and people, assent to power was given to the priest to lead a sacrifice anew. There were myriad abuses with multiple stipends for a singular Mass, and the more Masses that could be celebrated for one intention, the more they would be considered more. Jesuit scholar Robert Daly comments,

> Behind this was the . . . legitimate theological idea of the relatively infinite merits of the communion of Saints, that the church possesses a relatively infinite and inexhaustible storehouse of merit that can be drawn upon to help make atonement for the sins of its members. . . . Behind all this was the deep-rootedness of mercantile and legal-transactional metaphors and ideas when thinking about grace and redemption. In effect to a reform-minded Christian, the church was turning into a dirty human business in which salvation could be bought and sold; and the key and most valuable item being sold was the Sacrifice of the Mass.[23]

In conjunction with this development of the eucharistic rites within the ritual system were the theological reflections concerning the atoning work of Christ for which there is an interplay (*lex orandi/lex credendi*[24]) with the performance of the rites, auditorily, visually, kinesthetically, gustatorily, and sometimes olfactorily. In the clearest of terms, Frank Senn

21. Daly, *Sacrifice Unveiled*, 146, 183.

22. Senn, *Christian Liturgy*, 247–48.

23. Daly, *Sacrifice Unveiled*, 147.

24. *Ut legem credendi lex statuat supplicandi* (So that the law of supplication might ground the law of believing).

reminds us that "medieval theory and praxis was laid over new words to give them a new interpretation,"[25] i.e., what was popularly understood, which was really what was misunderstood was often different than the text of the canon. A perfect example is that the canon never claims to offer up Christ. It offers up the church.[26] But the actions told another story.

Within the juxtaposition of what was written, what was performed, and what was received, Luther examined the eucharistic actions and sacerdotal beliefs of his day, beliefs through which the eucharistic body had become separated from the ecclesial body. The understanding that we are brought into contact with the Risen Lord, the concern of the early fathers as we are gathered at his table, was far from the center of scholastic thought.[27] This dismemberment had been growing for centuries. Through such a praxis, he drew particular conclusions about the eucharistic texts. Inside Luther's hermeneutic, "[his] intention was to set [allegorical] instruction aside in favor of a more actual and historical interpretation of the Lord's Supper derived solely from the words of Christ."[28] Luther attempted to recover the sheer "giftedness" of the gift of the union of God with his people, which he believed was being held captive by what he experienced as the ecclesial power of Rome. This sense of sheer gift was lost for him in what was a reversal of direction between God's grace to humankind. He was also concerned that, "in the doctrine of transubstantiation, philosophy was allowed to override the biblical witness, [and that] transubstantiation failed to respect the logic of incarnation, on which the sacrament is based."[29] With a working hermeneutic of justification by faith (with a side of *sola scriptura*) as the central purpose of a liturgical gathering (rather than doxology), he understood hearing the scriptural words that speak justification (with the elements present) was absolutely necessary to return the Mass to its proper direction. So he truncated the text of the Roman Canon according to his understanding of what was necessary for the liturgy to clearly express this

25. Senn, *Christian Liturgy*, 248.

26. Senn, *Christian Liturgy*, 248.

27. Dennis C. Smolarski, *Eucharista: A Study of the Eucharistic Prayer* (New York: Paulist, 1982), 42.

28. Senn, "Martin Luther's Revision," 106.

29. Brett Salkeld, *Transubstantiation: Theology, History, and Christian Unity* (Grand Rapids: Baker Academic, 2019), 2–3. It is also important to remember that Luther's view of transubstantiation was heavily influenced by nominalism, which "had become overgrown with superfluous miracles, beginning with the annihilation of the bread and wine, something Thomas had explicitly rejected." Salkeld, *Transubstantiation*, 147.

justifying truth. Worship forms were overhauled according to his theological/doctrinal understandings (*lex credendi* certainly preceding and overpowering *lex orandi*) so that the new or adapted liturgical forms would express such doctrine, creating right and proper belief in the hearers. "Faith comes by hearing" (Rom 10:17a NKJV). Right doctrine became the pinnacle, and worship became the place to teach such doctrine.[30] To strengthen the pedagogical aspect of the liturgical gathering, the first hymns written were catechetical in focus.

Part of the wrong answer was that he took only the words that were recorded with the biblical narratives that tell about the event of the Last Supper. Unfortunately, he did not use the words that Jesus would have actually prayed (most likely in Aramaic) when he blessed (*berekah*) the bread and wine. Hear now the familiar words in Hebrew:

> *Baruch atah, Adonai Elohenu Melech haolam, hamotzi lechem min haaretz.*
> *Baruch atah, Adonai Elohenu Melech haolam, borei p'ri hagafen.*

> Blessed are you, O Lord, our G-d, King of the universe, who brings forth bread from the earth.
> Blessed are you, O Lord, our G-d, King of the universe, creator of the fruit of the vine.

Luther went back to the words "This is my body. This is my blood. . . . Do this as a memorial to me," but he did not go back to the rite.[31] He only went to the biblical narrative, the written text that contained the command with

---

30. We see this play out in later generations of Lutheranism. A prime example is what happened in 1811 in Sweden when King Gustav introduced a new handbook for Lutheran worship. He "openly said that the meaning of worship was to educate unsophisticated people and teach them the thoughts of the Enlightenment. The congregation was assumed to be there to listen and join in the hymns, now pedagogically corrected in the new hymn book. The eucharistic order was radically changed. The concept of prayer was abolished. The preface was omitted and a lengthy exhortation was introduced leading to the words of institution though the sursum corda remained. The reading of the words of institution became nothing more than a bible reading." Nils-Henrik Nilsson, "Eucharistic Prayer and Lutherans: A Swedish Perspective," *Studia Liturgica* 27 (1997) 176–99, esp. 180.

31. While in the East, the eucharistic prayer was often called the *anaphero* (I carry up, I offer in sacrifice), in the West it was sometimes simply called "the action" (*incipit canon actionis*) or "the prayer." The reference is not to speaking or proclamation, but to ritual action. Philip H. Pfatteicher, *Commentary on the Lutheran Book of Worship: Lutheran Liturgy in Its Ecumenical Context* (Minneapolis: Augsburg Fortress, 1990), 156.

a promise, but missed the initial act of the only-begotten Son's thanksgiving and then of sacrifice to the Father.[32]

By so doing, he missed the consecratory nature of the *berekah*, the prayer over the bread and wine, which is simultaneously "praise of God stated in the third person, like the creedal forms in Christian liturgies (Luke 1:68; Eph 1:3; 1 Pet 1:3)."[33] He missed that the institution narrative was like a shortened Seder haggadah, which explained the sacred meal.[34] As Jews recall what God has done to set us free, there is always an eschatological edge, for inside the memorial meal there is not only memory, there is, as the Christian gospel hymn sings, "Strength for today and bright hope for tomorrow, / Blessings all mine, with ten thousand beside."[35] In thanksgiving we are one with all that God has made. The prayer of thanksgiving is the consecration, and it is a prayer which blesses and praises God,[36] so that faith

32. "Sacrifice is not something that, in the first instance, begins as an activity of human beings directed to God, and then, in the second instance, become something that reaches its goal in the response of divine acceptance and bestowal of divine blessing in the cultic community. Rather sacrifice in the New Testament understanding—and thus in its Christian understanding—involves, so to speak, three 'moments.' The first 'moment' is the self-offering of the Father in the gift, the sending, of his Son. The second 'moment' is the unique 'response' of the Son, in his humanity and in the Spirit, to the Father and for us. The third 'moment'—and only then does Christian sacrifice begin to become real in our world—consists in the self-offering of believers in union with Christ by which they share in his covenant relation with the Father. The radical self-offering of the faithful is the only spiritual response that constitutes an authentic sacrificial act according to the New Testament (Rom 12:1)." Edward J. Kilmartin, *The Eucharist in the West: History and Theology*, quoted in Daly, *Sacrifice Unveiled*, 8.

33. Pfatteicher, *Commentary*, 157. When the *verba* is used without any other prayer, or even the dialog, the opportunity for the congregation to participate in a remnant of this blessing, the third pair of lines in the dialog ("Let us give thanks to the Lord our God. / It is right to give him thanks and praise"), is lost.

34. "In the dynamics and structure of the Eucharistic Prayer, the instituting words of Jesus are an 'embolism,' i.e., an insertion into an already existing prayer structure that is basically Jewish, but now Christianized, table prayer of blessing. As such the words of institution not only constitute the key element that gives specifically Christian meaning to what is fundamentally a Jewish prayer, they also take their meaning from their place and function within that prayer." Daly, *Sacrifice Unveiled*, 17. Stubbs also comments, "Supersessionism and anti-Judaism have suppressed the imagination of scholars, who for centuries ignored the Jewish roots of the Eucharist." David L. Stubbs, *Table and Temple: The Christian Eucharist and Its Jewish Roots* (Grand Rapids: Eerdmans, 2020), 13.

35. Thomas O. Chisholm, "Great Is Thy Faithfulness," Hymnary, 1923, st. 3 (https://hymnary.org/text/great_is_thy_faithfulness_o_god_my_fathe).

36. "If we go back further into history, to the development of the Christian Eucharistic prayer out of the genre of the Jewish *berekah*, it will be seen that the whole act of

is renewed as we look forward to all the "next year[s] in Jerusalem." When it comes then to Jesus's Last Supper with his disciples what some of us see and hear is Jesus's last will and testament, something that not only takes place in the present, but also directs us to the future, and the benefits to come from that will. But the last supper is not the first Eucharist. The first Eucharist does not occur until Sunday evening on the road to Emmaus, when the Risen Christ and his companions recall not only the immediate narrative but the ancient one as well, all the way back to Moses and the prophets, all the way back to the creation itself. "Blessed are you, O Lord, our God maker of all things."[37] In this setting of the evening meal, reminiscent of the haggadah, he who promised paradise to a thief a cross, is bringing Cleopas and his companion to taste of that promised paradise to come.

In Luther's restructuring of the canon, based on the flattened text, the polysemous nature of the texts in their performative doxological context was ignored, and so in many ways the liturgical gathering was stripped of both its epiphanous nature and its eschatological vision. Unfortunately, within such strictures (justification as *the* primary lens), the pastiche of biblical texts which we know as the words of institution were treated as a Bible reading[38] even though in 1523 they came off a *Qui pridie* clause, so technically they still could be considered part of a prayer, but they were not performed in a supplicatory way as they had once been in the early church,

---

thanksgiving was regarded as consecratory. We read in 1 Tim 4:4–5: 'For everything created by God is good, and nothing is to be rejected if it is received with thanksgiving; for then it is consecrated by the Word of God and prayer.' Thanksgiving serves to consecrate everything created by God. . . . In this light it would seem that in the primitive Eucharistic celebration, which probably had as its setting an actual community meal comparable to the Jewish Seder, the Institution Narrative took the place of the *Haggadah* as an explanation of what was happening. When the Eucharist was celebrated apart from the setting of a community meal, the new Christian Haggadah or prayer of thanksgiving was inserted into the Christian *berekah* or prayer of thanksgiving said over the bread and wine. It would seem, therefore, that the Lutherans discarded what was most primitive in the Eucharistic tradition, namely the act of thanksgiving, and retained what was secondary." Senn, "Martin Luther's Revision," 107–8.

37. Lutheran liturgy now has the option of praying such a blessing at the offertory, one which, "in increasing contact with the broader Christian tradition, and suggesting a reinterpretation of Christian sacrifice as the self-offering of the church (Rom 12:1–2) has introduced a simple offertory prayer." Pfatteicher, *Commentary*, 155.

38. Ironically, as a pastiche of the multiple accounts, the *verba* is technically not a Bible reading because there are already multiple layers of interpretation. In a sense it is a homiletic interpretation, especially with the addition of the phrase "which is given for you."

but simply as proclamation. Indeed, Luther gave the words of institution the same chanting tone as he had given the gospel. Luther may have wanted to move away from the metaphysical concepts of the scholastics, but he did not have the means to do so, so he and subsequent generations of Lutherans (and other heirs of the Reformation) became locked in as inheritors of the same type of argument clothed in their own subtle forms. This understanding of the *verba* as proclamation only left them doing just the opposite of what their theology wanted to express. In the mode of performance, the Reformation pastor, speaking the words of Christ, is still "confecting" the sacrament. While it remains a mystery (in, with, and under), it is the pastor's voice (although he may not have been understood to have undergone an ontological change), the pastor's voice that still is the guardian and en-actor of power, rather than by supplication to or invocation of the Holy Spirit.[39] In the words of Walter Bouman, "A prayer of thanksgiving does not make the eucharist our work instead of God's gift."[40] Luther was right to say that the direction of the rite was wrong, but what he missed was that the command to do this is ever within the context of Jesus's prayer. He technically kept the *verba* within the prayer in the *Formula* as it flowed from the preface. And was followed by the Lord's Prayer in the *Formula* (but preceded the admonition in the *Deutsche Messe*). And Jesus, our great High Priest, is still praying, still blessing. His work, the work of the triune God, is ongoing, and thus we call upon the Holy Spirit. And as we pray in the eucharistic prayer, "Join our prayers to those of your servants of every time and place and unite them with the ceaseless petitions of our great High Priest until he comes again."[41]

There is simply a liminality to prayer that has the potential to open one up to transformation to a new and deepening faith.[42] This is why in a

39. "It is not the presider who consecrates, the presider, speaking solemnly in the name of the assembly, petitions the Holy Spirit to consecrate the assembly and the Eucharistic gifts—notice the order—so that we, the assembly may become the true body of Christ offering ourselves with Jesus (for the force of this prayer to make us one with and part of Jesus's self-offering) to the Father." Daly, *Sacrifice Unveiled*, 18.

40. Walter R. Bouman, "Worship and the Means of Grace," in Ralph R. Van Loon, ed., *Encountering God: The Legacy of Lutheran Book of Worship for the 21st Century* (Minneapolis: Kirk House, 1998), 29.

41. Inter-Lutheran Commission on Worship, *Lutheran Book of Worship* (Minneapolis: Augsburg, 1978), 90–91.

42. "The condition of being on the way, which is the fate of the human subject, is not an aimless wandering in a desert waste without landmarks. In fact, eminently 'objective,' of the symbolic order. This law is made concrete in a process, the process of symbolic

full eucharistic prayer we pray for the transformation of the assembly as well as for the transformation of the gifts.[43] In fact, the transformation of the gifts is for the sake of transformation of the assembly.[44] I can still be overwhelmed as celebrant when using the so-called eucharistic prayer of Hippolytus, whose epiclesis prays for both the assembly and the gifts: "Send your Spirit upon these gifts of your church; gather into one all who share this bread and wine; fill us with your Holy Spirit to establish our faith in truth, that we may praise and glorify you through your Son Jesus Christ."[45] We cannot blame Luther for missing this, since by the late Middle Ages, the epicletic prayer happened at the offertory,[46] which was imbued with commercial and transactional intentions. But if we take Luther's forms, especially his *Deutsche Messe* as the template for all time, we, too, will continue the same error.[47]

---

exchange, which is properly structured and structuring in that it contains the *rules of the game* without which play cannot begin for lack of mutual understanding." For the "marvelous exchange" we call grace to take place, a liminality of an "arch-sacramentality" must exist. Louis-Marie Chauvet, *Symbol and Sacrament: A Sacramental Reinterpretation of Christian Existence* (Collegeville, MN: Liturgical, 1995), 99–100.

43. "Our written liturgies and our genuine receptivity to eucharistic practice have progressed at a greater pace than our eucharistic theology. . . . [Liturgical renewal] draws heavily from the texts and practices of the early church. However the eucharistic theology that still shapes Protestant churches and finds its way into basic theological text books often centers on reformation era points of division about the Eucharist. . . . Our eucharistic imagination—the thoughts, forms, metaphors, and theological substructures through which we view our performance of the Eucharist—is insufficient for comprehending the written liturgies and communion prayers that are commonly used." Stubbs, *Table and Temple*, 10.

44. "The transformation of an assembly, or of any of its members, into the Body of Christ is not something that does or can take place in anything resembling a 'magic moment.' Such a transformation can, at best, only begin in the here and now, and it can become complete only at the Eschaton." Daly, *Sacrifice Unveiled*, 182.

45. Scholars have come to some consensus that this eucharistic prayer was refined through a period of two hundred to three hundred years, with the *verba* coming as one of the later additions. See Bryan D. Spinks, "The Apostolic Tradition and Liturgical Revision," in Robert W. Prichard, ed., *Issues in Prayer Book Revision* (New York: Church Publishing, 2018), 209–10.

46. It is the context of the prayer, not the prayer itself ("Come, thou sanctifier, almighty, everlasting God, and bless these sacrificial gifts, prepared for the glory of thy holy name"), which is filled with the language of sacrifice that becomes so problematic for the Reformers. The prayer can be found in Thompson, *Liturgies of the Western Church*, 67.

47. "Luther's emphasis shifted sharply from appreciation of the action of the whole church to a concept of individual experience in the reception of the Sacrament. His most radical action, and the most questionable, was his omission from the heart of the

In my prairie churches there were always a few folks who would rarely come to communion because they understood themselves to be unworthy. Had the Eucharist been framed in prayer, where they were asking God for this gift of faith and new life, the outcome might have been different. By using the words of institution apart from the sacred frame of a eucharistic prayer, the church was telling the liturgy rather than liturgically expressing the narrative of God's saving love in a way that could abruptly awaken the hearers to the fact that we were not the center of the universe. Scholasticism used the liturgy as its mean to overcome "the breach that constitutes us as subjects."[48] We see this in everything from the veneration of relics to the prescription of manual acts that supposedly mimic what Jesus would have done at the Last Supper. The Reformers' use of proclamation for the *verba* apart from the context of a Trinitarian eucharistic prayer paradoxically had this same ritual agenda of the medieval church, which used the Mass as an allegorical drama: the turning of absence into presence. This is simply one more mutation of the genre of a religion of doubt, an older form of fundamentalism. Do we trust the formula rather than the God who hears? Article 7 of the Formula of Concord rejects the recitation of the minister as having the power to consecrate (i.e., confect). *However, reciting/proclaiming the words of institution alone does not safeguard against this understanding.*[49] Have we found a new magic? If Luther wished to free liturgical rites from magic he risked yet instituting another magic. In the twentieth century, French Roman Catholic liturgical theologian Louis-Marie Chauvet would comment on this problem, calling it "the magic of the word which believes it can change the world by its own manna."[50] There was a loss of the sense that "the mystery of the Eucharist is spread out across the whole Eucharistic Prayer and its accompanying ritual action, and that it cannot be atomized

---

communion service of all the prayers of commemoration and thanksgiving and limiting of liturgical material at this point to the Lord's Prayer and the Words of Institution. No other Christian liturgy had ever done this. In later years none but Lutherans—not all of them—followed Luther in this drastic procedure." Luther D. Reed, *The Lutheran Liturgy: A Study of the Common Liturgy of the Lutheran Church in America* (Philadelphia: Muhlenberg, 1947), 80.

48. Chauvet, *Symbol and Sacrament*, 172.

49. Theodore Tappert, ed., *The Book of Concord: The Confessions of the Evangelical Lutheran Church* (Philadelphia: Fortress, 1959), 481–86. Lutherans, in essence, gave the pastor the role of *in persona Christi* without *Christi capitis ecclesiae*. The *verba* alone, out of the context of the eucharistic prayer, sets the pastor/priest as above the assembly as mediator, a role that belongs to the Son. See Daly, *Sacrifice Unveiled*, 15–16.

50. Chauvet, *Symbol and Sacrament*, 326.

or located merely in one part, such as the Words of Institution."[51] The external signs of scholasticism have found a new wardrobe, but a dead body is still a dead body, and that is where Lutheran liturgy has been fixated since 1526. Like those who walked to Emmaus, until we let go of our desire to see a dead body, we will miss the living one who is known to us in the breaking of the bread.

And knowing the living One who come to us is the inheritance. The *beneficium* comes to us by means of *sacrificium*.[52] The overwhelming joy of the gift comes to us in thanksgiving, in the sacrifice of praise, because the paradoxical way in which this happens is the giving of thanks for who God is and for what God has done, is doing, and promises to do as well as for who we were made to be, our identities as creatures among God's many beloved creatures. "We confess in act"[53] that we are, in that moment, trusting God for what he has promised to do in making all things new. This sacrifice of praise, this prayer of thanksgiving, is the living out of God's desire for us and it is how we honor God, much like the Shema. As Father Schmemann once proclaimed, there is "nothing we can do, yet we become all that God wanted us to be from eternity when we are eucharistic."[54] We may speak many words, but we are the subject of the living Word in prayer.

Like Luther, we can look at inherited liturgical texts and make edits, good or bad, right or wrong, and I believe it is imperative to spend as much time living with the performance practices of any rite as deeply as we look at the texts before we make many changes. Liturgical texts are like road maps. They may give us an idea of the territory, but they do not necessarily bring an awareness to the many layers of terrain. It is in the landscape of performance (performative doxological eucharistic exegesis of the living Word) that we have the possibility to encounter beauty. As my friend Gordon Lathrop once said, "Manner has everything to do with meaning." The "how" becomes the "what," because we are not just disembodied talking heads. It's like my early experiences in the synagogue where nothing was considered too lavish, too extravagant, or too joyous. This is the opposite of minimalism, and this doesn't mean lavish in terms of economic opulence.

51. Daly, *Sacrifice Unveiled*, 150.

52. Yes, this is clearly in contrast to Luther's separation of *beneficium* and *sacrificium*. Martin Luther, *Word and Sacrament II*, ed. Helmut T. Lehmann and Abdel Ross Wentz, trans. Frederick C. Ahrens (Philadelphia: Fortress, 1959), 311–16.

53. Chauvet, *Symbol and Sacrament*, 341.

54. Alexander Schmemann, *For the Life of the World* (Yonkers, NY: St. Vladimir's Seminary Press, 1973), 45.

For a number of years my shul was in a storefront in a Long Island strip mall. But when the Torah was brought through the congregation and we kissed the tallis of the patriarch of the family and, reaching out, touched the sacred scroll as it passed by, we were transported, because the word of God was in our midst. Or when I was in La Isla, a *colonia* on the edge of Guatemala City where El Salvadoran refugees lived in cardboard shacks and walked down a steep ravine to wash their meager clothes along the rocky shores of the river. The church was made of tin and scraps of lumber, the paraments were torn shreds of grocery store plastic bags. We knelt in the mud to receive the Eucharist, mangy dogs running in and out, the scent of diesel fumes and garbage filling the air, and we knew our lives depended upon his body put into our hands, his blood poured in our mouths.

This is what Chauvet and others would call an arch-sacramentality, "the place where the believing subject comes into being." So much of this was lost in the centuries leading up to the Reformation, and so much of it has remained lost, and not just for Lutherans. But maybe now as we lean toward each other in conversation, regardless of what the sign over our congregations and seminaries might read, as we come to love one another, and listen and participate, we may yet discover that in worship as in love, sacrifice is not a work as it is done for the sheer joy of doing it.[55] Theodore Jennings says in his closing section on the rhythm of love in *Life as Worship: Prayer and Praise in Jesus' Name,*

> In the togetherness of prayer and praise we may discern the twin aspects of love: desire and delight. These correspond to the absence and the presence, the need and the gift, of the other. As a life of love, our existence is suspended between desire and delight.... Prayer and praise follow this same pattern. We wait and yearn and therefore pray for that time when our prayer will be transfigured into praise.[56]

Eucharistic worship transforms desire into delight by the sacrifice that is no sacrifice: love. Neither Luther nor his adversaries could see this, but both his right/rite questions and his wrong answers can serve to open our eyes, so that one day, the whole *oikumene* will feast in joy, in love, and in eternal thanksgiving.

---

55. While in these divisive times, we are formally in an "ecumenical winter," there is yet a longer arc of hope leaning toward spring.

56. Theodore W. Jennings Jr., *Life as Worship: Prayer and Praise in Jesus' Name* (Grand Rapids: Eerdmans, 1982), 138–39.

Between Form and Norm: Assessing the Evangelizing Potential of Balthasar's Theology

By Carolyn A. Chau

I FIRST ENCOUNTERED THE theology of Hans Urs von Balthasar during my doctoral studies at Regis College, the Jesuit faculty of theology at the University of Toronto. Like many, I discovered a refreshing passion and honesty in his work. Balthasar's description of neo-scholastic theology in terms of sawdust resonated, and the experience of reading Balthasar was, in contrast to neo-scholasticism, deeply moving. As I read *The Glory of the Lord*, *Theodrama*, and most especially *Prayer*, I found myself compelled repeatedly to set the book down in silent wonder at God's profound love for us or to utter a prayer of praise and thanksgiving for God's beauty, mercy, and majesty. Balthasar's ability to gesture toward the unfathomable depths of God's love for humanity and to articulate the way in which Christ reveals the depths of God's being as triune Love to us brought me literally to my knees. I was drawn to Balthasar's use of the metaphor of drama to provide an account of the human-divine relationship and to describe the escha-tological character of history. I appreciated the dynamism and existential realism of his vision of salvation history, which showed that we are always already in the life of God by God's gracious initiative and God's total self-giving love. Our loving response to divine revelation indeed occurs on the stage of life that has already been set by the triune God, with the Father as playwright, the Son as actor/protagonist, and the Spirit as the director.

Reading Balthasar wasn't all doxology and wonder, certainly. There were experiences of feeling perplexed, by his account of woman, for example, and the extremely confident clarity and precision that pervaded his theology of states of life in *The Christian State of Life*, and some of his discussions of the relationship between Christ and his church in terms of the relationship between Christ and Mary, especially as his ecclesiology emphasized the spousal relationship between Christ and church. However, the most distinctly jarring experience I had of reading Balthasar was Balthasar's treatment of other religions in the first volume of *The Glory of the Lord*. While his account of other religions is not as simplistic as a typology of other faiths into which Balthasar merely slots different forms of revelation in places at varying relative distances from Christianity, which alone contains the truth of Christ, Balthasar moves through various revelations across cultures to show that all instances of truth are but refractions of the unparalleled truth and beauty of Christ, in a way that can cause a contemporary Catholic to worry a little about triumphalism. Although I did not then and nor do I now consider myself to be a religious pluralist, something about Balthasar's mapping of the strengths and limitations of revelation found in other religions brought about noticeable affective dissonance within me bordering on disagreement. Nonetheless, here was a thinker who loved Christ and Christ's church and sought to help us all to fall in love with both again to bring about a more compelling Christian witness in the world. I was hooked.

Just to situate myself as a thinker, I'd like to clarify that I am not a Balthasar scholar. While I've written and published on Balthasar's ecclesiology and theological anthropology, it is the faith-culture question of contemporary Catholic mission in secularized societies that was and remains my area of chief concern and research. With regard to mission to secular societies, I believe that ethics, including the church's inhabiting of the ethical sphere, plays a crucial role in the mediation of God's Word to the wider world; hence the title of my paper, which I can imagine may sound a little cryptic, but indicates the way in which I engage the thought of Balthasar, namely, within the ambit of the question of contemporary Christian mission. I hope the "Form and Norm" part of the title will become clearer as the paper progresses.

The question before us is, what did Balthasar get wrong, in the light of what he got right? I address this question as follows. In part 1, I elaborate further what I take to be what Balthasar gets right, particularly in the area of ecclesiology. Part 2 discusses what I think Balthasar gets wrong or is at least problematic in his work. This section of the paper focuses on what seem to be dimensions of epic or totality that manifest themselves in certain areas of theological reflection. Part 3 presents an assessment of the evangelizing potential of Balthasar's theology through an analysis of the aforementioned problematic aspects of his theology refracted through the broader appreciation of Balthasar's chief insights for mission today.

PART I: What Balthasar Gets Right

Balthasar gets a lot right. He is right that God's love and beauty are excessive and unimaginable by the human mind alone. He is right that there is nothing that persuades and attracts as much as Love itself, which is given to us by a totally self-giving God in Jesus Christ. He is right that every instance of beauty in the world is a refraction of the divine glory that is Jesus Christ, and it is in Christ that all things achieve their deepest dimensions of being. As Ben Quash says, for Balthasar all things are comprehensively transformed and illumined by the particularity of Christ.[1] Balthasar is right that there is no place from which to see and to encounter God except from within the context of already being in a dramatic relationship with God.

Balthasar aptly describes the human relationship with God as one of radical dissimilarity and asymmetry: that God's love initiates the relationship, God's love makes the relationship possible, God's infinite freedom is what guarantees finite freedom, and our similarities to God will always be less than the dissimilarity we creatures have to our Creator. He is right that the heart of the church and the true authority of the church lies in the witness of the saints more than it does in popes. He is right that love engenders personhood more so than an intellectual act of self-reflection. That love, not self-conscious rationality, is the engine of personhood, and we are first set on the way of becoming persons as babes bathed in the warmth of our mothers' smiles. That our being, like that of the Trinity, is fundamentally relational (like the Trinity) rather than individualistic, and that we achieve personhood in and through enacting our mission. Balthasar also clarifies more ably than most the way in which the church forms us for mission, and hence personhood, and that God is found incomparably in Christ's church and her sacraments (but also in the beauty of the created order).

Homing in on Balthasar's awareness of the cultural situation in the West for mission, he is right that the legacies of Kant, Hegel, and Nietzsche

---

1. Ben Quash, *Theology and the Drama of History* (Cambridge: Cambridge University Press, 2005).

must be addressed for the church to find itself on firmer ground in modernity, and that the anthropocentric turn and cosmological approach are inadequate. Many have noted the way in which Balthasar's attention to the arts and literary arts especially is deeply important for theology (see Anne Carpenter). And there are some subtleties of Balthasar's ecclesiology that I find deeply insightful for the Catholic Church today as she seeks to follow God's Word. In *Bernanos*, his work on ecclesial existence, Balthasar names the need of the church to listen. As an Ignatian theologian, he exemplifies the practice of discernment. And he clarifies that even with a work such as *The Office of Peter and the Structure of the Church*, the goal is less to defend structure as primary ecclesial mode than as necessary for the life of the church. The truest foundation of the church is her Marian dimension, the recognition that the church emerges from the side of the crucified Christ and receives her life only from him.

Above all, I am struck by the simplicity and acuity of Balthasar's insight that love alone is credible and must be perceived. He writes, "If God wishes to reveal the love that he harbors for the world, this love has to be something that the world can recognize, in spite of, or in fact in, its being wholly other. The inner reality of love can be recognized only by love."[2] This is the core, one might say, of Balthasar's vision of mission. And because love is by its nature self-donating, humble, kenotic, it is not so wholly incomprehensible that God might give himself, in and through the church, in a way that people can "see." Love recognizes love. Balthasar provides a clarification of the ground that makes the human perception of divine love possible. Simply put, the conditions for the possibility of perception of love are there in God's gift of the church, Mary, and the Bible:

> This originally justified relationship of love (because it does justice to the reality) in itself threads together in a single knot all the conditions for man's perception of divine love: (1) the Church as the spotless Bride in her core, (2) Mary, the Mother-Bride, as the locus, at the heart of the Church, where the fiat of the response and reception is real, (3) the Bible, which as spirit(-witness) can be nothing other than the Word of God bound together in an indissoluble unity with the response of faith.[3]

The church is, on Balthasar's account, a clear gift of God to the world, as is Mary, the heart of the church, who teaches the church, and through the

2. Hans Urs von Balthasar, *Love Alone Is Credible* (San Francisco: Ignatius, 2004).

3. Balthasar, *Love Alone Is Credible*, 78–79.

church all of humanity, how to listen to and respond humbly and joyfully to God. The Bible, similarly, is a concrete, tangible expression of the intimate love between God and humanity, the embodiment of God's self-gift and humanity's response of faith.

Balthasar elaborates more fully in his analysis of faith in the first volume of *Herrlichkeit* (*The Glory of the Lord*) what allows humans to perceive God from the subjective side. He outlines the two traditions in contemporary theology that have dominated the discussion. On the one hand, there is the neo-scholastic reading of faith that sees faith as a kind of cognitive assent, in the first instance, to the signs that establish the divine authority and authorship of Christian revelation. Balthasar, like many others, rejects the neo-scholastic extrinsicism whereby "the events of saving history stand in an external relation to the truth which is revealed. They could have been other without affecting the substance of the *revelatum*."[4] This account of divine signs is positivistic in its account of historical truth: it is the truth of sacred history merely because it happened that way, not because there is a necessity to that history given by revelation itself. On the other hand, there is the reception of Augustine and Aquinas in modern Catholic thought by thinkers such as Maurice Blondel and his followers, who follow the great Christian theologians of the tradition in affirming that the "dynamism of the cognitive spirit is determined by its innermost disposition to press on to the vision of God, so much so that God's self-revelation and the elevation and grace required for the perception of his inner mysteries appear at the final stage in the perfecting of the structure of the created mind."[5] It is the light of faith (*lumen fidei*), given by God (part of God's active deed of self-revelation), that allows love to recognize love. Here, the problem Balthasar detects is a potential overemphasis on the knowing subject such that the measure of revelation is, ultimately, the noetic capacities of the subject and again, not revelation itself. We know, of course, that for Balthasar, revelation, Love itself, is the measure of what is believable. Balthasar's retrieval of beauty helps to clarify the depth-dimension of God. The capacity to see the Christ-form and to recognize the fittingness of the Form to the Godhead is by virtue of Love itself: God reveals himself *in* Christ, and all of us exist in the kenotic spaces between the persons of the Trinity. We are beings made

4. John Riches, "Balthasar and the Analysis of Faith," in John Riches, ed., *The Analogy of Beauty: The Theology of Hans Urs von Balthasar* (Edinburgh: T&T Clark, 1986), 52.

5. Hans Urs von Balthasar, *The Glory of the Lord*, trans. Erasmo Leiva-Merikakis (San Francisco: Ignatius, 1982), 1:148–49.

in and through Love, and Balthasar's theology helps us to recognize that we are protagonists within the drama of Love and it is our task, the Christian task, to share this good news, that we are all participants in the great drama of love between God and humanity.

Balthasar's awareness of the centrality of love in Christian claims and to the credibility of the gospel message is his greatest contribution to theology. He gives us a theology that brings out the truly vital, passionate character of salvation history, refusing to shy away from the self-emptying, sacrificial acts at the heart of Love and the salvation of the world. His famous (or infamous, depending on how one views it) account of Holy Saturday simply highlights the way in which Balthasar reveals the *passio* and the depths of Christ's love, and that this is what all Christians are called to share, to enact, as participants in the drama of salvation. Love is the name of God, Love is the name of the meaning and purpose of our lives, and Love empties itself for the other. And it is only in Christ that we can see truly the Love that is God.

So, this is my evaluation of what Balthasar gets right: the need for Love to be perceived and, as a corollary regarding mission, the need of the church to make visible the kenotic love of Christ for the world. But what is happening, then, when humans are, seemingly, no longer capable of perceiving/seeing the Form? Nietzsche's incisive observation about the profoundly oblivious indifference of the last men—"'God is dead, and we have killed him,' they say. And they blink"—seems to be a perfect description of the present moment in many parts of the North Atlantic West. While it is true that there are inadequacies with the neo-scholastic account of faith and the *nouvelle theologie* account, which fall prey respectively to the charges of an extrinsicist account of sacred history and a subjectivist account of revelation, I wonder how much Balthasar can truly answer the question of widespread cultural blindness that our contemporary secular culture in the West poses to the churches. Balthasar's missionary proposal, it seems, involves Christians pointing to Christ as the one who alone reveals the Trinitarian depths of God. But what then of a culture that fails to see this God who gives himself "without remainder" and yet is ever more mysterious? Certainly, one answer Balthasar gives is the classic one given by tradition. Our inability to see God has to do with the limitation of human sin. Balthasar discusses the failure to perceive Love. Love is perceivable, but our culture's failures to perceive love have to do with human sin. And his nuance is, importantly, that we cannot see the Form because we have lost the capacity to contemplate. This emphasis on the necessity of contemplation for the human-divine encounter is also part of what Balthasar gets "right." It should be noted, too, that his exhortation to contemplation is not encouragement of an esoteric spiritual practice for the uniquely skilled or gifted, but that contemplation is, ultimately, a matter of recognizing that God discloses himself to us, offers himself to us, in Jesus Christ and is thus available and accessible to all who make themselves vulnerable to divine grace and love.

Part II: What Balthasar Gets "Wrong"

There are many who would give a succinct and even strident answer to this question. Balthasar is abysmally wrong on gender, they would say, and his gender ontology must be rejected as it funds the patriarchy that is killing the contemporary Catholic Church and Christianity more generally (this view is held, for instance, by Karen Kilby). From another direction, some (e.g., Alyssa Pitstick) contend that Balthasar's account of God's will to save all must be named heresy. In my view, Balthasar's gender ontology is not wrong tout court, though I would admit that it is not problem free. Nor is he a heretic for laying out a proposal for the credibility of God's universal salvific will.

Underlying the many critiques of Balthasar that have been launched by feminists on the left or conservatives on the right, however, is a suspicion that Balthasar has said too much, has overreached theologically with his claims about what we can know about both God and humanity.

In my opinion, Ben Quash says it best when he claims: Balthasar's great problem is that even as he argues for a dramatic account of history that properly reflects the dynamism of God in Jesus Christ, Balthasar nonetheless himself falls into the epic mode of theologizing he so decries. I find this to be a fair analysis of the ultimate problem with certain aspects of Balthasar's theology: they are rather too "certain." This can come across as ontologizing in a way that overlooks historical reality. Whether it is the actual, historical subjugation of women to men or the ways in which Christianity has been a colonizing religion that shows little respect for the religious other, some of Balthasar's theological vision can, as Quash says, cause both subjects and structures in Balthasar's theodrama to undergo a kind of "freezing" that in fact undermines the unfolding of drama—and, I would add, the unfolding of mission.

In his 2005 book *Theology and the Drama of History*, Quash argues that on the one hand Balthasar has shown us why a theodramatic approach to history best illuminates the deepest convictions of Christian theology: that God is deeply interested and involved with humanity. On the other hand, although Balthasar criticizes both Hegel and Barth on their respective failures to narrate history dramatically, Balthasar's emphasis on *indifference* in human subjects makes Marian receptivity and obedience the dominant notes of fulfilled personhood and sanctity. This then controls the drama of history in human subjects in abstract and universalizing ways that are problematic. Quash bolsters his claims that there are these peculiar elements of closure and foreclosure in Balthasar's theology by careful analysis of the ways in which Balthasar reads texts at times in ways that seem to predefine where God is and how God is acting in the story. Quash puts the critique in Balthasar's own terms: Balthasar fails to maintain *the supra-structural* way in which God is, and this is evident in some of his treatments of Scripture, such as the book of Job. Quash believes that all the problematic elements come to a head in Balthasar's account of Holy Saturday, which Quash describes as taking place in epic or "remote" time. The problem is at bottom, a failure, according to Quash, to lift up ethical time and existential space. The smoking gun of epic is always that it moves spatially rather than temporally.

While I find it hard to quarrel with the centrality of *indifferencia* in Balthasar, which he learned from the founder of the Society of Jesus, St. Ignatius of Loyola, I can appreciate Quash's observation that it can sometimes seem as if freedom in Balthasar is in service of obedience, tout court, and of course that obedience is ecclesially mediated. In contrast, Barth's account of freedom is more existential and more along the lines of obedience for the sake of freedom. But while Quash sees freedom as the litmus test virtue for the dynamism of a theology, for Balthasar, Ignatian indifference is, ultimately, a case of obedience and freedom coinciding in Love, which is the ultimate value—freedom being penultimate.

My great concern with Balthasar's slippage into the epic mode at different points in his theological corpus is, however, the way it endangers the evangelizing potential of his work. The examples that I find particularly problematic given our current cultural context are the highly confident sense of how all the world religions hang together—which Balthasar exegetes in *The Glory of the Lord* and more succinctly in *Love Alone Is Credible*—and the way in which the genders relate to one another as call and response in his gender ontology.

Other Religions

In the first volume of *The Glory of the Lord* Balthasar discusses revelation as found in other religions. Balthasar there treats religious traditions such as Buddhism, Taoism, and Judaism in both the context of subjective truth and objective truth. His aim is to show that wherever there has been religious experience, that experience, in its luminosity, ultimately reveals the face of Christ as God. Interestingly, in these sections of *The Glory of the Lord* that underscore the way in which Christ is the true center of all religions, Balthasar acknowledges the merit of recognizing other religions with their gods.[6] However, the burden of this section of the theo-aesthetics is to show that objectively, from the object as it gives itself in experience, Jesus Christ is the true revelation of the glory of the Lord, and all other forms of religious faith are merely approximations in their articulation of who God is. Regarding followers of Taoism or the Hindu faith, Balthasar states:

> Let us take the example of a youth greatly enthused by the teachings of Lao Tzu. . . . Just in such a way, Hindu seekers for wisdom are convinced that it is only by the mediation of a guru, whose higher powers they cannot and will not dispense with, that they will be able to attain to the reality held out by their teacher's doctrine.[7]

In the same section he writes,

> When one fixes one's glance on the figure of Christ, can one really place him next to Buddha and Socrates as another "teacher of wisdom"? One should do this only if at the same time one realizes the much greater distance that separates him from them. . . . The analogy with the disciple of Lao Tze can also help to disarm a related objection.[8]

Balthasar narrates the experiences of followers of other religious founders to show the incomparable character of Christ as revelatory of God's being. He does this in the context of providing revelation's own evidence, the Form of Christ, for the truth of Christian faith, unearthing here the experience of subjective attunement to the Christ-form that throws into relief the contours of the Christ-form.

6. Hans Urs von Balthasar, *The Glory of the Lord*, trans. Erasmo Leiva-Merikakis, 2nd ed. (San Francisco: Ignatius, 2009), 1:177–81.

7. Balthasar, *Glory of the Lord*, 2nd ed., 1:177.

8. Balthasar, *Glory of the Lord*, 2nd ed., 1:180.

It is understandable that Balthasar depicts the other religions as lacking what is only complete in the revelation of Christ—the burden of *The Glory of the Lord* is to lay out how, in actively searching for the glory of the Lord in all forms of revelation, he could find it only in an unsurpassed and unequivocally true and exemplary way in the Christ-form. Balthasar's expressed purpose in *The Glory of the Lord* is to re-narrate what he learned about what comprises a masterpiece, the timelessness of a work of true beauty (his central concern in *Apocalypse of the German Soul*, he notes in *Epilogue*), in the key of one who has found God's true glory in Christ and Christ alone. It is also true, as Anthony Sciglitano's rich study of Balthasar's treatment of Judaism shows, that Balthasar's account of God's first covenant reveals an approach of fundamental Christian hospitality to other religions.[9] And yet, it is also reasonable to note that even with the robust theological and philosophical underpinnings Balthasar provides to articulate the uniqueness of the Christ-form in comparison to other exemplars of revelation or religious exemplars, the effect of this reading of other religions on Catholic mission for many living in pluralistic cultures today is not one of attraction but, quite possibly, repudiation. This is likely because without putting the work into understanding Balthasar's theology, with its deeply kenotic Christology, it is too easy to misread his theology of religions as exclusivist, and the exclusivist reading flies in the face of inclusivity, which forms part of the ethical aesthetic of many twenty-first-century Westerners, in particular young adults. (It is harder to see or hear the more nuanced point that Balthasar, committed to the Logos, sees the Logos as giving intelligibility and coherence to the logoi found in various cultural expressions. Instead, due to the typologies that have dominated theology of religions, it is too easy to perceive an undesirable triumphalism in his Christocentric thought.)

Gender

Balthasar understands man (male human beings) primarily as an agential force and an initiating, animating being, and woman as answer, response, also an agent, but an agent who responds to man and thereby brings about fruitfulness in her being as answer. Balthasar acknowledges that both

9. Anthony C. Sciglitano Jr., *Marcion and Prometheus: Balthasar Against the Expulsion of Jewish Origins from Modern Religious Dialogues* (New York: Herder and Herder, 2014).

initiator and response are fruitful, and therefore equal actors in the drama, but he also qualifies that woman is an "answering fruitfulness" in a way that makes it hard to deny, as much as he tries to do so, that there is a kind of subordination in the role of woman vis-a-vis the role and telos of man. Balthasar is even quite direct in naming the secondary role of woman to that of man. In addition to the qualities of receptivity and obedience that Balthasar exalts in his theology in general, and his account of woman, in particular, feminists attuned to the structural challenges that all women face qua woman are understandably disturbed by his theology.

I am less concerned that Balthasar's gender theory reproduces patriarchy than feminists who have typically criticized Balthasar's gender ontology for its pragmatic implications for social justice in the arena of gender. I do not read Balthasar as seeking to bolster patriarchy, but rather as challenging a fundamentally patriarchal mentality that takes man (*Dasein*) as self-sufficient in his power and powerful in terms of his agency (Promethean even). Balthasar replaces the ideal of human authenticity as power with the ideals of active receptivity, humility, and responsiveness à la the paradigmatic response of woman, and of Mary in particular.

However, I am concerned that, as with Balthasar's account of other religions, Balthasar's rather well-defined account of the relations between the genders does not reflect the kenotic, humble, self-giving love of a church that listens and accompanies sinners. Instead we seem to have a church that defines and orders.

This leads us to the broader question of where Balthasar situates ethics. This question of ethics is related to the challenge of whether Balthasar's theology can adequately explicate and address secular Western culture's inability to see the Form today. On the one hand, it is probable that Balthasar would state that the problem is precisely that the West has reduced Christianity to an ethic when what it needs is to see that the heart of discipleship is encounter with Christ. Balthasar often speaks of ethics in a similar vein to the critiques he aims at anthropocentrism or activism. In the *Prolegomena* to the *Theodrama* (vol. 1), Balthasar considers the various attempts to renew Catholic theology in the wake of the deadening effects of neo-scholastic theology on Catholic thought. In addition to theology as event and theology as history, Balthasar criticizes the move to make theology over as *orthopraxy* over against orthodoxy.[10] As Matthew Levering reminds us,

10. Hans Urs von Balthasar, *Theo-Drama: Theological Dramatic Theory*, trans. Graham Harrison (San Francisco: Ignatius, 1988), 1:33.

Balthasar's caution about this approach is that "while it drags Christianity out of the scholar's study and sets it on the world stage where it is to act and prove itself, [it] abbreviates it to an ethics or a guide to human endeavour." Levering elaborates: "God's transcendent action in Christ goes missing. Christian action, too, becomes deracinated, because it is faith in God and his action in Christ (ultimately, self-surrender) that must govern Christian action. After all, human action is not on the same level as divine action: the latter accomplishes everything, even while inviting and requiring the participation of humans."[11]

I agree with Balthasar that all must refract the glory of God, namely Jesus Christ. Christ and Christian faith must not be subsumed under ethics, but ethics ought to be placed in proper context, as with all else, under the lordship of Christ, and reflect the divine glory of his love. However, I think there is something else being overlooked in situating ethics thus, which is that in the historical unfolding of the drama between God and humanity in many contemporary Western secular cultures, ethics has become, I would argue, the gateway or the roadblock to seeing Christ in Christ's church. It is not sufficient, then, to simply criticize the ethicization of theology or the turn to praxis in theology, because, in fact, ethics has permeated the sphere of the aesthetic. One might say there has been an *aestheticization of the ethical.*[12]

To put it another way: today, ethics is not just about ethics. Ethics is also doing important work in terms of ecclesial mission. It is often the case today, among those who reject the church and eschew participation in the life of the church, that they do so on ethical grounds. The grounds for rejection range from sexism in the church to ecclesial exclusion on other sociological grounds, including the exclusivity of Christian truth over and against all other forms of religious truth. If Balthasar is correct about how

11. Matthew Levering, *The Achievement of Hans Urs von Balthasar: An Introduction to His Trilogy* (Washington, DC: Catholic University of America Press, 2019), 108.

12. I believe there needs to be transformation of ethics from within: a christological ethic that invites people back into the communion of the Bride of Christ. Balthasar can be seen to lay the foundations for the development of such an ethic with his own theology, and Catholic ethicists such as Christopher Steck and Melanie Barrett have developed compellingly the implicit ethic that flows out of Balthasar's theology: an ethic that is illuminated from within by Christ, the concrete norm, and his example of obedience, humility, and self-surrender as Steck puts it. In the account Barrett gives of a Balthasarian ethic, it is an exercise of finite freedom that is invited into the dance with divine freedom first through the attraction of love's beauty. See Melanie Barrett, *Love's Beauty at the Heart of the Christian Moral Life* (Lewiston, NY: Edwin Mellen, 2009).

the Form must be perceived, there is also work for the church to do such that her profile is one in which the Form is perceived, and that means engaging in the discourse about norms differently, as a proposal rather than a pronouncement (for example). The beauty that invites some people into the body of Christ is not one of definitive answers per se, but the trust that they will be accompanied in their journey with God by the community of faith.

Rather than him being wrong, one might note that there seems to be something missing in Balthasar's theology on the point of culture: Does he grasp the way in which culture *shapes* our capacity to see the Form? And, related to this, can the gospel be clearly communicated using Balthasar's theology? One could argue that he does understand secular culture (indeed I have made this argument myself in the past), but that he judges that culture to be sick and so he tries to show what culture ought to be. Here it may be useful to consider the way in which a very different Catholic thinker, Charles Taylor, with his attention to the genealogy of modernity in the West and the moral ontology of the modern self (as a self-interpreting animal among other things), may provide a helpful complement to Balthasar. While not a mere accommodationist to modern culture, Taylor does note the peculiarities of the moral self in modernity, which include an orientation to benevolence and universal justice as well as a habit of what Taylor calls "strong evaluation" whereby values themselves are evaluated by the modern subject and placed in subjectively ordered hierarchies. How does the Form "break through" to these perceivers? I'm not sure it is, in the first instance, through showing what culture ought to be.

Assessment: What Balthasar Gets Wrong in Light of What He Gets Right

The best ecclesiological insights of Balthasar include the fact that the Christian life is a drama, that Christian love is kenotic, and the church plays a powerfully important role both in bringing the drama to its redeemed eschatological end and in failing to bring about humanity's participation in divine life. Christian existence requires of each member of the body of Christ a close following of Jesus, that the body be a body that listens as each saint listens to the call of Christ in her life.[13] The institutional church, while necessary, is not as fundamental as the church of love. Balthasar is right

13. Hans Urs von Balthasar, *Bernanos: An Ecclesial Existence* (San Francisco: Ignatius, 1996).

about the glory of Love as the clearest justification for Christianity, and that nothing persuades or attracts more than Love itself.

If we can lean into all these insights and work on reshaping Catholic ethics in a way that steps back from a wholesale embrace of Balthasar's definitive configurations of interreligious relating and the relations between the genders—which may be construed as rigid dogma that stands apart from the incarnate reality that is visible in Christ—to consider how the church's ethical posture might more fully embody those dramatic, attentive, discerning dimensions of Balthasar's ecclesiology, then there is still much in Balthasar to guide us in the present age. Balthasar isn't wrong tout court, but there are aspects of the way in which he does theology that can present a roadblock to what many Christians who have stepped away from the church seem to need right now. In our current secular age, there is a clear and distinct allergy to totality and, it must be said, certainty. While the culture may be wrong to repudiate knowledge, the church might be challenged in her complacency. And, as mentioned previously, Balthasar's emphasis on drama is an important and real corrective here to an ecclesiology of certainty. It is only the certainty of faith, hope, love, and trust that Christ's church must proclaim. It cannot be more than this without becoming self-righteous in a way that relativistic culture legitimately recoils at.

What is tragic about these epic or perhaps overly ontologized aspects of Balthasar's theology—and I do wish to caution that perhaps it is not even Balthasar's theology, as he was not a systematic theologian per se, but those who seek to articulate his thought systematically for theology of religions or sexual ethics, for example—is that Balthasar's theology includes much to fund a "being on the way with God" approach (especially in his critique of those who would situate God before us or God ahead of us as opposed to God beside us, which he raises in *Who Is a Christian?*). His dramatic, process, time-centered approach coexists awkwardly, however, with an equally robust emphasis on the perfection of Christian life and not the struggle of ordinary Christians (take evangelical counsels and secular institutes, for example). Perhaps some of this perfectionism or "completeness" underwrites his accounts of gender and other religions, in a way that resonates less as the beauty of Love incarnate and more as the garishness of totality.

If this is the case, then the apologetic value of his theology is weakened, as those who are keenly attuned to issues of justice may be "blinded" by his gender ontology and approach to other religions, which can overshadow the brilliance of his account of love, beauty, and drama. I do think this is an issue with the viewer, but can a brilliant theology be reconsidered such that, at least, it does not undermine itself by leaving itself open to such misinterpretation?

In a word, yes. In addition to highlighting the dramatic aspect of Balthasar's theological account of the divine-human relationship, there is the importance of underscoring the role of contemplation both as that which funds his theology and as the condition for understanding it. To do theology through contemplation is to go beyond critical analysis and to the heart of things, which is Christ himself, Love incarnate. From that vantage point, much if not all of what Balthasar says truly makes sense.

The significance of contemplation and its loss in our wider culture also helps to explain why the misinterpretations are so likely. There is a larger cultural mixing up of religion and ethics where all too often religion is reduced to ethics. As an aside, I believe that ethics is both the gatekeeper and the shepherd of mission, and so the more we can both reduce in theology aspects that bolster a rejection of the gospel on ethical grounds, and the more we can strengthen in a theology the ethical aspects that support love of Christ, the more we are going to see a capacity to see the Form of Christ in Christ's servant, the church. Concurrent with this need to make clearer the gestalt of the Christ-form in the church is the need to cultivate a contemplative spirit in the church and in the world.

In the meantime, I advocate for the importance of rescuing the Form from Balthasar's epic temptations. When one succumbs to the epic mode of theologizing, the range of things one says about revelation expands. I'm proposing a move to realize that more is under exploration than Balthasar might portray in his theology. I say this realizing that there are others for whom Balthasar is already too exploratory, too much of an author rather than a theologian for whom the primary task is not authoring the faith but simply transmitting it in fidelity to the tradition. In response to this criticism I would point to the profound humility and gratitude with which Balthasar speaks of doctrine as that which "accompanies" us.[14] Now, I am not advocating accommodation to current cultural norms tout court. Bodies are particular and religions are distinctive, and we can have relative clarity on both these sets of issues, but not as much clarity as Balthasar tends to claim. And this modesty I'm advocating is not a liberal modesty, but the modesty of a Christian who knows, ultimately, that all norms are,

14. Balthasar, *In the Fullness of Faith: On the Centrality of the Distinctively Catholic,* trans. Graham Harrison (San Francisco: Ignatius, 1996), 56–57.

at the end of the day, subject to the un-normed norm, the concrete norm of personhood, Jesus Christ. Jesus is a definite something, and our Nicene and Chalcedonian Creeds help us to name with some clarity the something that Christ is. So this acknowledgment that perhaps the church needs to take on more of the mode of an accompanist does not amount to compromise on who Christ is or a shift to a notion of norms as being ever-more plastic. Nor does it amount to an attempt to be deceptive or equivocal about the faith. But it does challenge those who would emphasize Balthasar's account of gender[15] or other religions to ask the question of how these emphases work to further the capacity of those today who are lost and seeking God, to "see the Form" in the church. How might the church today, inspired by Balthasar's Christocentrism, turn anew and ever more to the God who accompanies us as we seek to participate in his redemption of a broken world? How is God asking the church to accompany those who can no longer see the Form of Christ in the church because of the way Christian norms have been presented? How can we foreground our encounters with those who have left the church with an experience of the tenderness and mercy of the kenotic Christ rather than with the moral norms and well-defined expectations and definitions of truth that leave them only with the experience of being judged?

Coda

Let me conclude with a coda on mission in the papacy of Pope Francis. Pope Francis, in contrast to his predecessors, notably in not being a theologian by training or European, has tapped into something different; arguably, the truly dramatic aspect of Christian ecclesial life and mission that Balthasar often renders in his theology so beautifully. Consider, for example, the tremendous risk Francis is taking and the drama of faith that is involved in convoking a synod on synodality in which the whole people of God are

15. An important insight from Rowan Williams on the controversy surrounding Balthasar's gender ontology is that what's more importantly at stake in Balthasar's account of gender is whether and how it coheres with his Trinitarian thought: "how far sexual differentiation can be said to partake of the differentiation of the trinitarian persons, a differentiation in which there is no unilateral and fixed priority or derivation but a simultaneous, reciprocal conditioning, a pattern of identity in the other without remainder." See "Balthasar and Difference" in Rowan Williams, *Wrestling with Angels: Conversations in Modern Theology*, ed. Mike Higton (Grand Rapids: Eerdmans, 2007), 82–83.

being invited to share what they are hearing when they attend prayerfully, together, to the voice of the Holy Spirit in their midst. Whereas Popes John Paul II and Benedict XVI have arguably, in their own ways, focused on Balthasar's engagement of Nietzsche, and hence the question of truth and what has happened in the contemporary modern West to this question, as well as beauty and the good, Francis seems to recognize in a more poignant way the existential, dramatic, fleshly dimension of the goodness of God. His pontificate has shown that people need to experience the beauty of the church as the one who accompanies them along the way, in the flesh.

Concretely, this has issued forth in exhortations both official and unofficial to love divorced and remarried persons, our homosexual brothers and sisters, migrants and refugees, the poor, and the earth. Pope Francis's ecclesiology of joy, accompaniment, and encounter get at something I believe is urgently needed for the church's contemporary mission to the secular West. Personhood is the site of mission, but not personhood as a concept (this may do for theologians and philosophers), but personhood as an experience. Whether we decry it or celebrate it, experience is the lingua franca of modernity. So is subjectivity. These are not new insights. We all know this. Balthasar's genius as a modern Catholic thinker has been to transform these categories from within. Only in and through Jesus Christ can our experience and subjectivity be truly glorious, and glorious and fulfilled because they give glory to God.

In her essay "Doctrine and Praxis in Pope Francis's Approach to Evangelization," Melanie Barrett, a Balthasar scholar, notes:

> In contrast to John Paul II's conceptual use of doctrine, Francis utilizes doctrine primarily to animate practice. In so doing, he turns outwardly to the world first—focusing on the concrete needs of those who are poor, broken, or lost—so that the parameters of their existential situation can dictate the shape of the Church's response.[16]

This is a way, genuine concern for the poor, that people today seem to be able to grasp the Christ-form in their midst. As Todd Walatka, author of *Von Balthasar and the Option for the Poor*, has ably shown, this approach is not inconsistent with Balthasar's theology, but does require a kind of completion, as it is not fully worked out in Balthasar's theology and some ecclesial

16. Melanie Barrett, "Doctrine and Praxis in Pope Francis's Approach to Evangelization" in *Pope Francis and the Event of Encounter*, ed. John C. Cavadini and Donald Wallenfang (Eugene, OR: Wipf and Stock, 2018), 115.

leaders have not promoted it.[17] No doubt my analysis of Balthasar here is informed by my own current ruminations on what the church requires to be perceived as beautiful and credible in a secular age, as well as my sincere conviction that the Holy Spirit is ever with the church and ever will be. May the Form that so often radiates through the work of Balthasar radiate also through a church normed by the one, true, concrete norm, Jesus Christ.

17. Todd Walatka, *Von Balthasar and the Option for the Poor: Theodramatics in the Light of Liberation Theology* (Washington, DC: Catholic University of America Press, 2017).

The Place of Christology in Dogmatic Theology: A Critical Engagement with Wolfhart Pannenberg

By David Luy

THE DOCTRINE OF CHRIST occupies a unique position within the enterprise of dogmatic theology. Since the early nineteenth century, a significant number of influential theologians have insisted that Christology ought to determine the Christian's understanding of God to an extent that overshadows or perhaps even displaces every other epistemological input. In this paper, I reflect upon the place of Christology within dogmatic theology by engaging the work of Wolfhart Pannenberg (1928–2014). Pannenberg is a fruitful conversation partner, because although he is an heir to the Barthian tradition and thus emphatically stresses the centrality of Christ for theology, he also complicates the concept of a "Christocentric dogmatics" in significant and provocative ways. Pannenberg addresses the enterprise of Christocentric theology directly in an article published in 1975, which bears the title "Christologie und Theologie."[1] Pannenberg's approach to the topic is dialectical. In solidarity with the modern Christocentric movement, he affirms the aspiration for theology to renounce all knowledge of God except the knowledge that is made available to us in Christ, but he also chastens this impulse by stipulating a counterpoint principle. We cannot

---

1. Wolfhart Pannenberg, "Christologie und Theologie," *Kerygma und Dogma* 21 (1975) 159–75. In this essay, I will be referring to a subsequent printing of the article in *Gesammelte Aufsätze: Grundfragen systematischer Theologie* (Göttingen: Vandenhoeck & Ruprecht, 1980), 2:129–45.

know Christ rightly in abstraction from the God to whom he relates, and with whom he is identified.

Pannenberg does not set forth his counterpoint principle in order to repudiate modern Christocentrism. As we shall see, he remains zealously committed to the idea that Christian theology ought to derive its doctrine of God from the history of Jesus, and he concurs with the critical verdict espoused by other Christocentric thinkers that earlier approaches to dogmatic inquiry (classical and modern) are guilty of relegating Christology to an excessively marginal position and status. Despite his intentions, however, I suggest in what follows that Pannenberg's counterpoint principle is more profoundly subversive to the enterprise of Christocentric theology than he intends. By emphasizing that Christology is an embedded doctrine (i.e., a doctrine inextricably positioned within a particular, theological framework), Pannenberg effectively undermines the methodological demand expressed by many modern Christocentrists for theological reflection simply to "begin" with Christ. Pannenberg's contributions to this topic can be regarded as a "mixed blessing" because although his dialectical approach makes a significant contribution to the ongoing conversation concerning the place of Christ in dogmatic theology, he inadvertently obscures key implications for this topic which follow from his constructive proposal. Pannenberg intends his article as a modest course correction, which essentially upholds the cause of modern Christocentrism, but the inherent momentum of his argument supplies good reason to question that radical Christocentrism can provide a coherent methodological program for dogmatic inquiry.

My paper proceeds in three main sections with a brief conclusion. The first section introduces the rhetorical trope of "pure Christocentrism" and focuses attention upon a critical tension which this trope raises. The second section outlines Pannenberg's dialectical approach to the place of Christ in dogmatic theology. Here we will see that Pannenberg is mindful of critical tension and seeks to address it in a manner that does belie his radical commitment to the methodological priority of Christology in dogmatic theology.[2] Section 3 argues that, despite his intentions, Pannenberg's

2. For a more comprehensive exposition of Pannenberg's Christology, see Gunther Wenz, *Introduction to Wolfhart Pannenberg's Systematic Theology* (Göttingen: Vandenhoeck & Ruprecht, 2012), 138–65; G. G. O'Collins, "The Christology of Wolfhart Pannenberg," *Religious Studies* 3 (1967) 369–76; Roger Olson, "The Human Self-Realization of God: Hegelian Elements in Pannenberg's Christology," *Perspectives in Religious Studies* 13 (1986) 207–23; Frank E. Tupper, "The Christology of Wolfhart Pannenberg," *Exegetical Review* 71 (1974) 59–73.

dialectical proposal effectively calls the enterprise of Christocentric theology into question, at least as that enterprise is commonly presented and understood.[3] In the conclusion, I briefly identify a few significant implications of the engagement with Pannenberg for how we might reflect anew upon the place of Christology within dogmatic theology.

The Rhetoric of Pure Christocentrism

Modern enthusiasm for Christocentric theology is rooted to a great extent in the promise of a dogmatic system wholly purified of alien contaminants. At a time acutely sensitive to the limits of theoretical reason, and unsettled by the rise of biblical criticism, the prospect of a theological system more wholly determined by Jesus of Nazareth—and thereby less reliant upon philosophical speculations and heteronomous authorities—was bound to attract considerable interest.[4] The gambit of modern Christocentrism, in all its various forms, has essentially been that Christian theology can escape its precarious reliance upon dubious conduits of theological knowledge by subjecting its inquiries more comprehensively to strict, christological governance.[5] Christocentrism is an attempt to provide Christian theology with a more secure methodological footing, while simultaneously restoring the discipline to its proper subject matter—i.e., the God made known to us in the person of Jesus Christ.

What precisely does strict christological governance entail? Answers to this question vary considerably, even among thinkers who embrace the ideal of a "Christocentric theology" with equal zeal. For some, upholding the priority of Christ means abiding within a strict set of epistemological parameters. If it is to be "pure," this approach contends, Christian theology

3. It must be emphasized at this point that modern Christocentrism is a highly diverse movement, and the argument set forth in this essay is limited in scope to variants of the movement which embrace the rhetorical trope of pure Christocentrism. Earlier iterations of modern Christocentrism (such as expressed in the work of Friedrich Schleiermacher, for example) may exhibit other problems, but inasmuch as they do not advance the rhetoric of "pure" Christocentrism, such problems reside entirely beyond the purview of my present argument.

4. For a helpful account of the rise of modern Christocentrism which emphasizes this very point, see Eugene TeSelle, *Christ in Context: Divine Purpose and Human Possibility* (Philadelphia: Fortress, 1975).

5. Modern criticism also destabilized the tradition's confidence in Scripture for reliable theological judgments. See Michael C. Legaspi, *The Death of Scripture and the Rise of Biblical Studies* (Oxford: Oxford University Press, 2011).

must affirm *only* those dogmatic judgments about God that derive exclusively from Christology. As justification is by faith in Jesus Christ and not by works of the law (Gal 2:16), so genuine knowledge of God comes exclusively through Christ, and is not available to us through any other means.

The daring simplicity of this methodological posture bears an undeniable rhetorical power. And yet, despite its considerable influence within twentieth-century theology, the demand for what we might refer to as a "pure Christocentrism" produces an apparent dilemma. If the doctrine of Christ is to function as the exclusive starting point for theological reflection, how is the theologian to identify the particular understanding of Christ with which she ought to begin? A Christocentric system may claim to begin simply with Christ, but, of course, it inevitably begins instead with some particular *construal* of Christ. And this construal will not proceed from nowhere as a bare given, but must necessarily presuppose some conceptual frame of reference in relation to which identity of Jesus is located. Because of its formative contributions *to* Christology, it is difficult to see how this conceptual frame of reference can plausibly claim to be derived at the same time exclusively *from* Christology. Herein lies the crux of the dilemma. If Christocentrism is to be "pure," as the aforementioned rhetorical posture putatively demands, it must apparently begin exclusively with Christ and disavow other conduits of theological knowledge. And yet, how can theology claim to begin exclusively with Christ if every understanding of Christ is embedded inextricably within an interpretive horizon, which is not wholly derivable from Christology?

Pannenberg's Dialectical Christocentrism

Pannenberg's article addresses the dilemma of pure Christocentrism by reflecting upon the relationship between Christology and theology in dialectical fashion. Whereas many modern Christocentric thinkers are animated simply by a desire to avoid the error of subjugating Christology to an alien conceptuality, Pannenberg warns that a pitfall threatens theology on the opposite extreme as well if we fail to conceive of the relationship between Christology and theology with adequate nuance. Yes, theology must not subject Christology to a preformed conception of God (the characteristic error of classical dogmatics in Pannenberg's estimation, and of many Protestant liberals as well), but it must also avoid behaving as if the identity of Christ can be accessed apart from the theological tapestry within which

Jesus's historical life is embedded (a risk he associates with certain existentialist strains of modern Christocentric theology). In good dialectical fashion, Pannenberg expresses the guardrails necessary for sidestepping each of these pitfalls in the form of crisp assertions at key junctures in his essay. With respect to the first, he declares: "If God is only revealed through Christ . . . then the Christian cannot wish to have any knowledge of God outside of Christ."[6] With respect to the second, he states: "The man Jesus of Nazareth is not accessible [to us] without his God."[7] The dynamism of Pannenberg's proposal stems from the creative interplay which unfolds between these two impulses (i.e., the impulse toward pure Christocentrism; and the impulse to embed Christology within a robust, theological framework). The aim of this section is to explain how Pannenberg develops each of these commitments and sets them in dialectical relation one to the other.

Pannenberg's affirmation of the first intuition (i.e., the impulse to pure Christocentrism) is closely related to a sharp critique he levies against the classical theological tradition. Traditional dogmatics is guilty in his estimation of formulating its conception of God entirely in abstraction from the doctrine of Christ. Pannenberg is well aware of the fact that classical writers have much to say about the incarnation, of course, but he insists that such reflections are situated downstream of governing presuppositions about the nature of God which are derived from extra-christological means of knowing (e.g., philosophical speculations). Christology may be an important locus of attention within classical dogmatics, but theological reflection upon Christ is constrained by a theological architecture materially indifferent to the fact that God became human in the person of Jesus Christ.[8]

The marginal position occupied by Christology within traditional dogmatics creates two fundamental problems according to Pannenberg's analysis. We can refer to these as the "polarity problem" and the "dispensability problem," respectively. The polarity problem warns that a doctrine of God abstracted from the person of Christ will inadvertently undermine the conceptual feasibility of Christology. Because of its pre-christological

---

6. Pannenberg, "Christologie und Theologie," 2:129.

7. Pannenberg, "Christologie und Theologie," 2:130. "Der Mensch Jesus von Nazareth ist nicht ohne seinen Gott zugänglich."

8. Pannenberg, "Christologie und Theologie," 2:129. "In der tradionellen Dogmatik scheint das Verhältnis von Christologie und Gotteslehre klar bestimmt zu sein: Die Gotteslehre wird vorweg und unabhängig von der Christologie entwickelt, diese hingegen setzt die Gotteslehre und insbesondere die Trinitätslehre voraus, indem sie mit ihrem eigenen fundamentalen Thema, der Inkarnation des Gottessohnes, einsetzt."

starting point, the classical tradition relies heavily for its understanding of God upon trajectories of philosophical speculation, which set God's nature diametrically in contrast to finitude. The essence of God is understood through a systematic negation of creaturely limitations, and this renders the concept of divine perfection more or less synonymous with non-creatureliness. The eventual result is an oppositional account of the God-world relation that alienates God from the domain of history.[9]

Not surprisingly, ahistorical conceptions of divine perfection turn out to be infertile soil for christological inquiry in Pannenberg's estimation. Classical accounts of the incarnation strain to affirm the proposition that God became a human being in the person of Jesus Christ, but the effort is undermined at every turn by the more fundamental assumption (rooted in antique philosophy) that God and creation *cannot* be united, because they are separated from one another by an unbridgeable, ontological chasm.[10] As Pannenberg sees it, the enterprise of classical Christology was more or less destined to fail under these conditions.[11] And even if it succeeded in some purely technical sense (perhaps through a feat of virtuosic, philosophical sophistry), the underlying commitment to a conception of divine perfection that alienates God from history effectively ensures that Jesus of Nazareth *cannot* genuinely reveal the nature of God to us.[12] He is, after all, an agent wholly enmeshed within history. In short, the polarity problem argues that traditional dogmatics adopts a polarized conception of the Creator-creature distinction, and this conception effectively renders the prospect of a divine incarnation unthinkable.

The polarity problem leads directly to the second critique of traditional dogmatics, which animates Pannenberg's sympathy for pure Christocentrism; namely, the dispensability problem. By establishing core beliefs about God in abstraction from Christology, classical sources effectively render Christ superfluous (and thus dispensable) to a genuinely Christian

---

9. Pannenberg, "Christologie und Theologie," 2:133–34. See also 139.

10. Pannenberg, "Christologie und Theologie," 2:134.

11. Pannenberg is by no means the first to advance this critical argument. For a representative parallel, see Reinhard Schwarz, "Gott ist Mensch: Zur Lehre von der Person Christi bei den Ockhamisten und bei Luther," *Zeitschrift für Theologie und Kirche* 63 (1966) 289–351. For a closer examination of Pannenberg's assessment of two-nature Christology, see Christian Schönborn, "Aporie der Zweinaturenlehre? Überlegungen zur Christologie von W. Pannenberg," *Freiburger Zeitschrift für Philosophie und Theologie* 24 (1977) 428–45.

12. Pannenberg, "Christologie und Theologie," 2:132–34.

doctrine of God.[13] The life and teachings of Jesus may bear witness to some aspects of this classical understanding, but if the doctrine of God is established apart from Christology, it follows that Christ might theoretically be excised from Christian theology, and this excision would not require any substantive adjustment to the doctrine of God. Can a dogmatic system claim to be meaningfully Christian that effectively treats the history of Jesus as dispensable in this manner? For Pannenberg, the answer is obviously no.

Although Pannenberg's critical diagnosis focuses primarily upon the classical tradition, modern Christologies do not escape his rebuke. His critique bears superficial resemblance to the admonition expressed by many modern writers that theology should renounce its dalliance with speculative metaphysics and affix its gaze more completely upon the life of Jesus.[14] And yet, despite this apparent convergence, Pannenberg insists that early Protestant liberals (like Schleiermacher, for example) remain guilty of establishing their operative conception of God apart from the formative influence of Christology. For all their putative emphasis upon the history of Jesus, Pannenberg complains that many modern Christologies locate the theological significance of Jesus's life in relation to a generic conception of religious consciousness, which has little to do with history.[15] Christ may exemplify ideal human consciousness in relation to God, but the conception of God to which Jesus's consciousness is moored is not substantially derived from Christology.[16] This approach to Christology upholds the

13. Pannenberg, "Christologie und Theologie," 2:129. "Wenn Gotteserkenntnis auch ohne Christologie begründbar ist, dann muß sich letzen Endes die Frage stellen, ob die Christologie nicht überhaupt eine überflussige Hypertrophie christlicher Lehrbildung darstellt."

14. For a helpful engagement with these sources, see Michael Welker, *God the Revealed: Christology* (Grand Rapids: Eerdmans, 2013), 55–103.

15. Pannenberg explains that many modern Christologies dismiss Jesus's own view of God as a culturally conditioned objectification of religious experience. This means that in order to get at the true core of the matter, the theologian must interpret Jesus's discourse about God in light of her own religious intuitions and operate with the assumption that such religious experience is the essential taproot beneath the historically conditioned husk. Pannenberg, "Christologie und Theologie," 2:132.

16. In Schleiermacher's case, this presupposes a particular interpretation of how the preface relates to the material dogmatics sections within the *Glaubenslehre*. For a lucid expression of this interpretation, see B. A. Gerrish, *A Prince of the Church: Schleiermacher and the Beginnings of Modern Theology* (Philadelphia: Fortress, 1984), ch. 2. The notion that Schleiermacher begins his theology with general presuppositions concerning the nature of religious experience has recently been questioned by Robert Sherman and Maureen Junker-Kenny. See Robert Sherman, *The Shift to Modernity: Christ and*

importance of Jesus as a model for Christian piety, but, for Pannenberg at least, it still does not redress the fundamental problem that radical Christocentrism is meant to solve, namely, the subordination of Christology to a preformed conception of God. Here, as before, something other than the doctrine of Christ occupies the driver's seat within the task of dogmatics. And when Christian theology begins with a preformed conceptual understanding of God, that conception inadvertently undermines Christology (i.e., the polarity problem), and renders Christ superfluous to a Christian understanding of God (i.e., the dispensability problem).[17]

Specialists in the history of dogma may rightly object to various aspects of the narrative Pannenberg sketches here. For present purposes, it is important simply to notice that Pannenberg's embrace of radical Christocentrism flows directly from his critique of classical and modern dogmatics. In order to escape the polarity problem and the dispensability problem, theology must reverse its conventional sequencing of judgments. Rather than beginning with a preformed understanding of God and then turning to Christology in relation to that presuppositional substrate, theologians must resolve instead to begin with Christ and to conceive of everything else (God especially) from this privileged vantage point. Or again, as Pannenberg puts it: "If God is only revealed through Christ . . . then the Christian cannot wish to have any knowledge of God outside of Christ."[18]

The place of Christology in dogmatic inquiry appears clear and straightforward from this vantage point. If the article were to conclude at this juncture, it would seem that Christian dogmatics ought to be nothing

---

the Doctrine of Creation in the Theologies of Schleiermacher and Barth (New York: T&T Clark, 2005); Maureen Junker-Kenny, Das Urbild des Gottesbewußtseins: Zur Entwicklung der Religionstheorie und Christologie Schleiermachers von der ersten zur zweiten Auflage der Glaubenslehre (New York: de Gruyter, 1990); Maureen Junker-Kenny, Self, Christ, and God in Schleiermacher's Dogmatics: A Theology Reconceived for Modernity (New York: de Gruyter, 2020).

17. Pannenberg, "Christologie und Theologie," 2:132. "Für unseren Gedankengang hat sich indessen das vielleicht überraschende Resultat ergeben, daß die klassische Inkarnationschristologie und die moderne Christologie 'von unten' an einem gemeinsamen Mangel leiden, indem sie nämlich darin übereinstimmen, daß beide einen anders als durch die Christologie selbst erst zu gewinnenden Gedanken der Wirklichkeit Gottes schon voraussetzen müssen, damit die Christologie im eigentlichen Sinne überhaupt beginnen kann. Das bedeutet aber daß weder das eine noch das andere Verfahren es vermag, Gott als durch Jesus von Nazareth offenbar zu denken und also die Einheit von Gott und Mensch in Jesus zu denken. Man sollte meinen, das sei das eigentliche Thema aller Christologie."

18. Pannenberg, "Christologie und Theologie," 2:129.

but a series of unilateral extrapolations from Christology. And yet, it is precisely at this point that the second prong of Pannenberg's dialectic introduces an unexpected wrinkle. The Christian understanding of God may rightly begin with Jesus of Nazareth, but it is conversely true to say that the identity of Jesus is inextricably bound up with a particular understanding of God.[19] The doctrine of God must resolve to begin with Christology, but there is also a sense in which Christology must resolve to begin with the doctrine of God.[20]

As with his arguments in favor of Christocentrism, Pannenberg's impulse to embed Christology is motivated by theological pitfalls he wishes to sidestep. In this latter case, he is especially concerned to avoid a tendency to reductionism that the rhetoric of pure Christocentrism may inadvertently inspire. If the goal is to limit our knowledge of God *entirely* to what can be known exclusively through Jesus, what are we to make of those aspects of Jesus's life and teaching that express continuity with the social, religious, and intellectual context of the first century? Taken to its logical extreme, the aspiration for theology to disavow all pre-christological conceptual judgments could lead one to the rather strange conclusion that even the concrete particulars giving shape to Jesus's own life must be set aside in order to procure a thoroughly Christocentric theological perspective.[21]

This radical posture would surely exclude Jesus's own understanding of God, inasmuch as it is not wholly original to his consciousness but is, rather, an artifact of history thoroughly embedded within the thought patterns of first-century Palestine and continuous in many important respects with the theological outlook of Second Temple Judaism.[22] If the goal of pure Christocentrism is to eradicate every understanding of God which originates upstream of Christology, then Jesus's view of God must also be excluded. Pannenberg points out that a reductionist approach such as this can be regarded as viable only if one accepts the premise that Jesus of Nazareth is "entirely understandable" (*überhaupt verstehbar*) apart from

---

19. Pannenberg, "Christologie und Theologie," 2:130.

20. Pannenberg, "Christologie und Theologie," 2:134. "Der Gott Jesu ist nur durch den Menschen Jesu zugänglich, aber auch der Mensch Jesus nur von seinem Gott her."

21. Pannenberg, "Christologie und Theologie," 2:130. Pannenberg appears to have the thought of Rudolf Bultmann principally in mind at this juncture.

22. For a helpful examination of the relationship between early Christology and the thought world of Second Temple Judaism, see Crispin Fletcher-Lewis, *Jesus Monotheism* (Eugene, OR: Cascade, 2015), vol. 1.

the God to whom he continually relates.[23] Pannenberg asserts to the contrary, however, that this is quite impossible. We simply cannot comprehend Jesus in abstraction from his conception of God. For Pannenberg, Jesus's understanding of God, and his relation to God, are both what we might refer to as "identity constitutive."[24] As he states the point: "The man Jesus of Nazareth is not accessible [to us] without his God."[25]

So, despite his obvious enthusiasm for the enterprise of Christocentric theology, Pannenberg makes it clear with this second axiom that we must not construe "beginning with Christ" in a facile manner that overlooks the embedded nature of Christology. The doctrine of Christ is inextricably joined to an interpretive horizon, and we cannot surgically excise Jesus from that framework without fundamentally transforming, and thus eclipsing, his proper identity. What we need then, according to Pannenberg, is a reciprocal approach to the relationship between theology and Christology. Dogmatic inquiry must robustly affirm (with Barth) that God is only accessible to us through the historical person, Jesus of Nazareth; but it must also affirm that Jesus of Nazareth is only understandable in light of the God to whom he relates, and with whom he is identified.[26]

Pannenberg urges dogmatic inquiry to conceive of God and the world from the perspective of their union in Christ. This posture requires significant adjustments to the traditional conception of God, and also unsettles its operative understanding of history.[27] God and the world are not discrete entities effectively brought into relation after the fact. Christian theology must learn to conceive of both God and the world as teleologically ordered to unification in Christ.[28] This outlook leads Pannenberg to embrace

23. Pannenberg, "Christologie und Theologie," 2:130. "Voraussetzung dafür ist allerdings—neben einer wohl allzu großen Leichtgläubigkeit gegenüber den Argumenten der neuzeitlichen Religionskritik—daß der Mensch Jesus ohne Gott, ohne *seinen* Gott, überhaupt verstehbar ist."

24. For a fuller articulation of this point, see Wolfhart Pannenberg, "Die Aufnahme des philosophischen Gottesbegriffes in der frühchristlichen Theologie," in *Grundgragen systematischer Theologie: gesammelte Aufsätze* (Göttingen: Vandenhoeck & Ruprecht, 2011), 296–346.

25. Pannenberg, "Christologie und Theologie," 2:130. "Der Mensch Jesus von Nazareth ist nicht ohne seinen Gott zugänglich." It is also important to notice that this approach, by emptying Christology of its durable content, paradoxically offers to us a Christocentrism without Jesus Christ.

26. Pannenberg, "Christologie und Theologie," 2:131.

27. Pannenberg, "Christologie und Theologie," 2:138.

28. Pannenberg, "Christologie und Theologie," 2:135–36, 141–42.

a quasi-theogonic account history that echoes the view of German idealists such as Hegel and Schelling. With Ernst Troeltsch, Pannenberg insists that the history of religious representation in particular should be regarded as an extended, divine act that progressively actualizes the reality of God through time.[29] Because the union of God and creation is embraced as ontologically primary, it follows that the teleological realization of humanity through history is at the very same moment the teleological realization of God (albeit in a somewhat different sense that seeks to preserve a meaningful affirmation of divine aseity).[30] Pannenberg's constructive proposal deserves a much fuller exposition than is possible within the constraints of this essay.[31] My purpose at present is not to evaluate this proposal, but rather to assess whether Pannenberg can rightly claim to extrapolate his views exclusively from Christology as the essay from 1975/1980 seems to allege.

The Subversive Momentum of Pannenberg's Dialectic

Pannenberg's dialectical proposal yields a number of contributions that advance our understanding concerning the place of Christology in dogmatic inquiry. By emphasizing the embedded character of Christology, Pannenberg complicates the rhetoric of pure Christocentrism. The theologian cannot simply resolve to begin exclusively with Jesus, because she must first determine who Jesus is, and attending to this task of identification will inevitably involve recourse to an interpretive horizon of some kind. This is a critical insight. Pannenberg's approach likewise encourages a less dichotomized and more nuanced judgment concerning the place of Christology in dogmatic theology. Theologians should not behave as if we must inevitably choose between one of two unilateral approaches to the ordering of theological judgments—as if every dogmatic system necessarily begins *either* with God *or* with Christ. On the contrary, as Pannenberg makes clear, Christology and the doctrine of God relate to one another in a reciprocal manner, and each doctrine sheds critical light upon the other. Any attempt to transform the relationship from a state of interdependency

29. Pannenberg, "Christologie und Theologie," 2:138.

30. Pannenberg, "Christologie und Theologie," 2:144–45.

31. For a helpful engagement of these ideas, see Robert Jenson, "Jesus in the Trinity: Wolfhart Pannenberg's Christology and Doctrine of the Trinity," in *The Theology of Wolfhart Pannenberg: Twelve American Critiques, with an Autobiographical Essay and Response*, ed. Carl Braaten and Philip Clayton (Minneapolis: Augsburg, 1988), 188–206.

to a one-sided trajectory of influence will inevitably distort both theological domains.

Pannenberg does not offer these important adjustments in order to repudiate the project of radical Christocentrism. Certainly, he wishes to sidestep problematic extremes latent within the movement, but he offers his critical adjustments without ever relinquishing or renouncing the fundamental aspiration to establish a conception of God wholly grounded in the history of Jesus. In the remainder of this section I want to suggest that Pannenberg's dialectical proposal is more profoundly subversive to the enterprise of Christocentric theology than he recognizes. His emphasis upon the embedded character of Christology is meant to chasten potential excesses within the modern Christocentric movement, but the manner in which he remediates these problems effectively calls the very impetus to radical Christocentrism seriously into question.

It is important to recall that Pannenberg's positive case for Christocentric theology is motivated primarily by a critique of traditional dogmatics. He chastises premodern theologians for importing a preestablished understanding of God, and then constraining reflection upon Christ to the rigid parameters of that conceptual grid. From this vantage point, Christocentrism is necessary because it liberates dogmatic inquiry from a Procrustean bed. This general critique of the tradition is commonplace among contemporary advocates of Christocentrism, and provides powerful impetus to the methodological prioritization of Christology that pervades modern theology. Pannenberg's second dialectical principle creates an apparent problem for this way of thinking, however. If Christology depends for its intelligibility upon an interpretive horizon that Christology itself cannot provide, then the impulse to situate christological reflection within a theological horizon cannot automatically be dismissed as nefarious.

Once Christology is acknowledged to be an embedded doctrine, it no longer suffices as a critique of traditional dogmatics simply to observe that it relies upon an understanding of God that is not grounded exclusively in Christology. Pannenberg's counterpoint principle thus implicitly undercuts a critical assumption that galvanizes support for the cause of Christocentrism in the first place (i.e., the assumption that traditional dogmatics situates the person of Christ within a theological framework not derived from Christology, and that this is a very bad thing). The deeper question this line of argument raises is whether Pannenberg's dialectical principles can be embraced as complementary judgments (as he intends), or whether they should be regarded instead as contrary intuitions between which one must choose. Can we simultaneously affirm that a reciprocal relation exists between Christology and the doctrine of God, *and* that God is revealed to us exclusively in the history of Jesus?

Pannenberg offers a few hints for how we might reconcile these two, apparently antithetical claims. One possibility would be to insist that the impulse to embed Christology does not imply recourse beyond the doctrine of Christ because the interpretive horizon to which Jesus's life belongs is not an extrinsic frame of reference, but is itself ingredient to Christology. Thus construed, the embedding principle does not give license for dogmatic inquiry to deploy just any conceptual framework in service to christological reflection. In order to maintain a Christocentric approach, the theologian must limit herself instead exclusively to those theological points of reference that are directly implicated by the Christ event. For example, the doctrine of the Trinity can be regarded as ingredient to Christology because Jesus's relationship to God the Father, and to God the Spirit, is a constitutive feature of his personal history.[32] The same could not be said, however, for a conception of the divine attributes that relies upon the inferences of theoretical reason without reference to the history of Jesus.[33] From this perspective, Pannenberg's proposal coheres with the demand for a pure Christocentrism because situating Jesus in relation to the doctrine of God does subjugate Christology to an *extraneous* conceptual domain. Reflection upon God emerges naturally as one attends to the Christ event, because Jesus's view of God, and his relation to God are both constitutive of his distinctive identity.

This response to the objection is promising, but it leads to a demarcation problem. In order for the explanation to work, it must be possible neatly to differentiate between theological commitments that are ingredient to Christology and theological commitments that are not. How are we to differentiate between these conceptual domains in a nonprejudicial manner? The Christ event does not present us with an unambiguous line of demarcation with which we can identify its borders. The doctrine of God provides a good illustration of the problem. According to Pannenberg's

---

32. Pannenberg gestures in this direction in "Christologie und Theologie," 2:132–33.

33. This paragraph develops a line of argument to which Pannenberg hints on "Christologie und Theologie," 2:130–31. For an alternative assessment of the relationship between Christology and classical theism, see Joseph Thomas White, *The Incarnate Lord: A Thomistic Study in Christology* (Washington, DC: Catholic University of America Press, 2017), vol. 5; and Stephen J. Duby, *Jesus and the God of Classical Theism: Biblical Christology in Light of the Doctrine of God* (Grand Rapids: Baker Academic, 2022).

proposal, dogmatic inquiry must restrict itself entirely to the understanding of God that the history of Jesus inherently presupposes. And yet, as C. H. Dodd and others have shown, the account of Jesus's history to which the New Testament offers us access is inextricably embedded within a rich theological tapestry to which the entire canon of Scripture is apparently ingredient, inasmuch as early Christology consists to a large extent in the exegesis of Israel's Scriptures with respect to the life, death, and resurrection of Jesus.[34] And since the scope of the canonical witness thus accessed for christological use extends to encompass all of reality, before too long it will become difficult to rule out any conceptual domain whatsoever as extraneous to Christology.[35]

Pannenberg himself gestures in this direction at one point in his essay by clarifying that radical Christocentrism does not rule out "natural" knowledge of God, because all of creation and the whole history of humanity is included within the domain of Christology since the very fabric of reality is grounded in the communion of Father, Son, and Spirit.[36] This inclusive posture satisfactorily resolves the demarcation problem, but it does so apparently at the expense of modern Christocentric rhetoric in its most radical form.[37] For if *everything* is christological, what precisely does a commitment to Christocentrism effectively rule out? And here again, to the extent that Pannenberg affirms the appropriateness of situating the Christ event within a cosmic (even metaphysical?) frame of reference, it will be difficult for him to sustain the polemical case against traditional dogmatics that motivates his endorsement of radical Christocentrism in the first

---

34. See, for example, C. H. Dodd, *According to the Scriptures: The Sub-Structure of New Testament Theology* (London: Collins, 1965); Donald H. Juel, *Messianic Exegesis: Christological Interpretation of the Old Testament in Early Christianity*, Library of Early Christology (Waco, TX: Baylor, 2017); and Richard B. Hays, *Reading Backwards: Figural Christology and the Fourfold Gospel Witness* (Waco, TX: Baylor, 2016).

35. See, for example, the cosmic frame of reference for christological reflection in John 1; 1 Cor 8:6; and Col 1:15–18.

36. Pannenberg, "Christologie und Theologie," 2:134–35. "Ist, wenn es so steht, menschliche Gotteserkenntnis überhaupt unmöglich? Das war die Konsequenz der frühen dialektischen Theologie, und diese Konsequenz wäre unabweisbar, wenn Schöpfund und Mensch einfach außerhalb des Kreises des göttlichen Lebens, das Vater und Sohn miteinander verbindet, stehen würden. Enspricht aber eine solche Antithetik von Gott und Welt, Gott und Mensch, noch der christlichen Auffassung, daß die Schöpfung selbst durch den Sohn begründet ist und von dem Geiste lebt, der der Geist der Gemeinschaft des Vaters mit dem Sogne und des Sohnes mit dem Vater ist?"

37. Pannenberg, "Christologie und Theologie," 2:134–35.

place. Pannenberg thus appears to be caught in a dilemma. Either he must abstract Christ from the canonical horizon within which we encounter him (thus creating a demarcation problem), or he must expand the domain of Christology to such an extent that his critique of the tradition for moving beyond Christology no longer makes sense. In short, it seems that the impulse to embed Christology should lead Pannenberg to relinquish rather than simply to adjust the rhetoric of radical Christocentrism.

Conclusion

The purpose of this paper has been to reflect upon the place of Christ in dogmatic theology by engaging the work of Wolfhart Pannenberg. Pannenberg's dialectical proposal offers a nuanced reflection upon this question that rewards careful attention. My argument has especially focused upon Pannenberg's emphasis upon the embedded character of Christology. Whereas the rhetoric of radical Christocentrism urges us to begin resolutely with Christ, this counterpoint principle rejoins that the identity of Christ is not a bare given, but is joined inextricably to a particular, theological horizon. This suggests it is not actually possible to prioritize Christ while bracketing the interpretive horizon to which he belongs. Although Pannenberg outlines his dialectical proposal as a means of formulating a more nuanced form of Christocentrism, I have argued that his counterpoint principle effectively subverts the very enterprise of Christocentric theology as commonly understood.

A few significant implications follow naturally if my critical appropriation of Pannenberg's proposal is valid. It follows first of all that the rhetoric of radical Christocentrism does not work very well as a cudgel with which to disqualify alternative, theological points of view. If Christology is embedded within an interpretive horizon, then it is no argument against the classical tradition (or any other theological point of view for that matter) simply to observe that it situates christological reflection in relation to a conceptual frame of reference that is not explicitly derived from the doctrine of Christ. If Christology and the doctrine of God relate to one another in a reciprocal fashion, then we should not suppose that a non-christologically derived conception of God necessarily renders Christ "dispensable" to Christian theology. Such conceptions may function instead as the indispensable frame of reference in relation to which Christ's identity is properly recognized. When it comes to supplementary frames of reference beyond the explicit domain of Christology, the question should not be *whether* such frames can be tolerated, but *which* of the available options provides the most apt interpretive horizon for situating the identity of Jesus. For those who acknowledge the embedded nature of Christology, the use of some such frame will be embraced as inevitable; and despite the rhetorical tenor of much modern Christocentrism, it is best for dogmatic inquiry not to pretend otherwise.

How, or Better *Why*, I Changed My Mind on Infant Baptism

By Charles (Chad) Raith II

The Journey to Affirming Infant Baptism

I ENTERED CHRISTIANITY AT the age of twenty-one, and the tradition that mothered my faith was the Baptist tradition. I can recall the moving experience of being baptized during a Sunday evening service at First Baptist Statesboro in Statesboro, Georgia. I had actually requested the baptism, believing even then that it would mark a profound shift from the old to the new life. The Baptist tradition would continue to nurture my faith for many years to come. During my undergrad studies at Georgia Tech, where I studied industrial and systems engineering, I attended First Baptist Atlanta and sat eagerly under the teaching of Charles Stanley. That eagerness led me to attend seminary at Beeson Divinity School, studying under the pre-eminent Baptist theologian Timothy George. I would eventually become an ordained minister in the Baptist church and serve over the years as youth pastor, college pastor, deacon, elder, worship leader, and theologian in residence.

But in this journey another profound event occurred in my life: I had a son. We had our first son "dedicated" during a Sunday morning service at Dunbar Heights Baptist Church in Vancouver, British Columbia. Baby dedication, if you don't know, is (more or less) the Baptist corollary to infant baptism, or as J. I. Packer quipped to us as students at Regent College: it's dry infant baptism. Baby dedication is a way of recognizing the inclusion of the baby in the family of God and the church's commitment to help the parents raise the child in the ways of the Lord. Somewhat ironically the practice of baby dedication, along with studying John Calvin and the church fathers under Hans Boersma at Regent College, began turning my wheels about the validity of infant baptism. And by the time our third child was born six years later, we had accepted the practice of infant baptism and had all three baptized on the same day—the Sunday of the Baptism of our Lord—the oldest being six years, the youngest being two months. We have subsequently baptized our next three children as infants as well. (That's six kids if you've lost count.)

Let me acknowledge up front that with each infant baptism, not only was I and am I soberly aware that such a practice creates a deep fissure with the tradition that richly nourished my faith for so many years, but I am also mindful of the history of suffering undergone by those who stood against the practice in order to defend a more biblical Christianity as they understood it. While a number of examples could be given, the martyrdom of Michael Sattler in 1527 has come to stand out for me. His martyrdom, along with his wife's, became well known throughout much of Europe. Sattler was respected even by those who disagreed with his position; Martin Bucer and Wolfgang Capito, for example, "grieved" when they heard of his execution. Lutheran Gustav Bossert wrote of Sattler, "Sattler was not a highly educated divine and not an intellectual; but his entire life was noble and pure, true and unadulterated."[1]

So knowing I was breaking with the ecclesial mother of my faith and betraying those in my broader heritage who had laid down their very lives for this issue, how, and maybe more interestingly *why*, did my view of baptism change? I begin the story with John Calvin, not because his argument changed my mind (it did not), but because the very weakness of his "biblical" justification for infant baptism helped me realize that the argument for infant baptism could not be a strictly "biblical" (i.e., purely exegetical) argument, nor more than (so I came to realize) the argument against it. That is, Scripture alone would not solve the issue. If someone was already convinced infant baptism was wrong, citing various scriptures in favor of it would remain unconvincing; and if someone was already convinced infant baptism was right, pointing to the absence of explicit affirmation for it in Scripture would remain unconvincing. The real shift that took place was less about understanding certain scriptural passages differently (though

1. For the story of Sattler's martyrdom and responses to it, see William R. Estep, *Renaissance and Reformation* (Grand Rapids: Eerdmans, 1986), 203–4.

that did occur) but rather *how* I went about reading those passages *in light of the church's reception of those passages*. That is, the fundamental reason for why I changed my mind on infant baptism is because I changed my view of the relationship between Scripture and tradition.

John Calvin's Argument and Its Weaknesses

While the Anabaptist movement—a movement that denied infant baptism—never obtained the same number of adherents as other Reformation traditions, it attracted enough followers and gained enough momentum that eventually, at the request of William Farel, Calvin inserted himself in the situation and in 1544 released his "Brief Instruction for Arming All the Good Faithful Against the Errors of the Common Sect of the Anabaptists,"[2] hereafter called the "Brief Instruction." Already in his original 1536 *Institutes* Calvin had demonstrated his disagreement with various Anabaptist beliefs, such as on the nature of the church, the oath, taxes, civil authority, and infant baptism, and his 1539 expansion of the *Institutes* evidences even greater familiarity with Anabaptist teachings. The 1544 "Brief Instruction," however, marks Calvin's "definitive" refutation of Anabaptist beliefs.[3] In the "Brief Instruction" Calvin walks through the booklet *Seven Articles* sent to him from Farel—some surmise this booklet from Farel to be the *Schleitheim Articles* attributed to Michael Sattler. For our purposes, I am only interested in the first article, on baptism, which states:

> Baptism ought to be given to those who have been instructed in repentance, who believe that their sins have been blotted out by Jesus Christ, and who want to walk in His resurrection. Consequently it ought to be administrated to those who request it for themselves, not for infants, as is done in the pope's kingdom.[4]

While there are many elements to Calvin's refutation of this article, his argumentative approach for affirming infant baptism is to appeal to Scripture as affirming the practice. The cornerstone of Calvin's biblical argument is how he understands God's covenant with His people, which

2. *Corpus Reformatorum: Ioannis Calvini Opera quae supersun omnia*, ed. W. Baum et al. (Brunswick: Schwetschke & Filium, 1863–1900), vol. 7, cols. 51–52. The English translation used for this paper is *Treatises Against the Anabaptists and Against the Libertines*, trans. and ed. Benjamin Wirt Farley (Grand Rapids: Baker Academic, 1986).

3. Calvin, "Brief Instruction," in *Treatises*, 23–24.

4. Calvin, "Brief Instruction," in *Treatises*, 44.

includes God's promise to be the God of the believer's children, and how he understands the continuity between baptism and circumcision. The logic is fairly straightforward: Abraham first believed in God's promises and subsequently received circumcision as a sign of inclusion in God's promises. Yet the covenant promises included being the God of Abraham's offspring, and his children received circumcision. The covenant promises of Old are the same as that of New, with circumcision and baptism as signs of the same covenant realities. Thus in the new covenant adults first believe in the gospel and are subsequently baptized. But the promise is also to a believer's children, and thus the children of believers are also to be baptized.

I will not dispute the merits of Calvin's logic in his "Brief Instruction," for it seems sound *if* you accept the hermeneutical premises. But I judge the premises uncompelling, and thus I find Calvin's argument for infant baptism being ultimately unconvincing to anyone who is not already disposed to accepting the practice of infant baptism.

Let me first highlight some unique elements to his hermeneutic by briefly—too briefly—examining the thought of his predecessors who explored a connection between circumcision and baptism. Cyprian's Epistle 64 is one of the first writings to make any ado around the connection between circumcision and infant baptism. But in his response to Bishop Fidus, the issue for Cyprian is whether baptism should be done on the eighth day; Cyprian does not use circumcision to justify infant baptism per se.[5]

Augustine makes the connection between circumcision and baptism even stronger. He writes in "On Marriage and Concupiscence," "Ever since circumcision was instituted amongst the people of God, which was at that time the sign of the righteousness of faith, it availed also to signify the cleansing even in infants of the original and primitive sin, just as baptism in like manner from the time of its institution began to be of avail for the renewal of man."[6] While Augustine connects circumcising infants and baptism, the emphasis is on the power of each to effect renewal; the circumcision of infants is not used to *justify* the baptism of infants.

Peter Lombard devotes book 4, distinction 1, chapters 6–10 of his *Sentences* to circumcision, couching circumcision as an "old testament" sacrament and reflecting on the similarity and difference between Old

---

5. Cyprian, Ep. 64, in Alexander Roberts et al., eds., *Ante-Nicene Fathers* (Buffalo, NY: Christian Literature Publishing, 1886), 5:56.

6. Augustine, *On Marriage and Concupiscence*, in Philip Schaff, ed., *Nicene and Post-Nicene Fathers*, 2nd ser., trans. Peter Holmes and Robert Ernest Wallis, 4th ed. (repr., Peabody, MA: Hendrickson, 2004), 5:292.

Testament sacraments and New Testament sacraments like baptism. Lombard asserts that while both circumcision and baptism provided for the remission of original and actual sin, circumcision did not impart the helping grace necessary to live a transformed life, unlike baptism, which does. Again, Lombard is not using the practice of circumcising infants to justify the practice of baptizing infants.[7]

While Lombard connects circumcision and baptism in general terms of how Old Testament sacraments relate to new testament sacraments, Thomas Aquinas makes the connection between circumcision and baptism even stronger. In *ST* III, q. 70, a. 1, Aquinas asks whether circumcision was "a preparation for, and a figure of Baptism," and argues that it was. The connection between the two is now more explicit than in either Cyprian, Augustine, or Lombard. But when unpacking the similarity and difference between the two, Aquinas evidences the difficult nature of understanding their relationship. In a rare moment in the *Summa*, he explicitly sets forth the position he himself had held years earlier in his *Sentences* commentary and disagrees with it, admitting he has since changed his mind. After refuting Lombard's position and his own previous position, Aquinas concludes that the locus of difference between circumcision and baptism is not so much what happens in regard to grace—he concludes that both of them remove original and actual sin *and* impart grace—but in how they impart forgiveness and grace. Circumcision imparts grace due to the faith a person has in the sacrifice to come. Circumcision is a sign of that faith and has no power in and of itself to impart grace apart from the faith of the person. Baptism, however, because the sacrifice of Christ has already occurred, itself has the power to impart grace, and this impartation is to be received by faith of the recipient. Thus, in circumcision, the key to making circumcision efficacious is the faith of the recipient. In baptism, the baptismal waters are themselves efficacious due to the sacrifice of Christ, and the effects are received by faith.[8] Once again, there is no justification of infant baptism based on the circumcision of infant children.

A couple of observations about this all-too-brief historical overview are in order. First, in the whole development from Cyprian to Augustine to Lombard to Aquinas, only a single passage of Scripture is ever cited as connecting circumcision and baptism, and that is Col 2:11–12. And not

---

7. Peter Lombard, *The Sentences*, bk. 4, trans. Giulio Silano (Toronto: PIMS, 2010), 6–9.

8. Thomas Aquinas, *Summa Theologiae* III, q. 70, a. 4.

even this verse is always utilized by these thinkers.[9] To be sure, arguments made by Augustine and others refer to various Scripture passages when discussing infant baptism, but the conclusion to these arguments requires connecting dots—sometimes numerous dots—that Scripture itself does not connect. As Westminster Seminary professor Dennis Johnson puts it in an article describing his own journey to accepting infant baptism, "I came to recognize that there is no New Testament text that answers point-blank the question, 'Should believers have their children baptized?'"[10]

Second, in none of these discussions do the authors use the connection between circumcision and baptism to *justify* infant baptism. In an article explicitly asking whether children should be baptized (*ST* III, q. 68, a. 9), Aquinas does not mention circumcision at all in his argument.

Third, while the authors affirm a similarity between circumcision and baptism, they also emphasize the difference between the two, rooted in the difference between the Old and New covenants. None affirm the level of continuity between the two covenants that Calvin does.

These observations are relevant when we judge the merits of Calvin's justification of infant baptism in the "Brief Instruction." Judged from the point of view of someone approaching the argument already *rejecting* infant baptism, one weakness of his argument is theological: his emphasis on the continuity between circumcision and baptism and the way he justifies infant baptism by appealing to circumcision are both unprecedented. Calvin, I note, was on occasion labeled by his opponents a "Judaizer" due to his strong emphasis on the continuity of the Old and New Testaments; he was accused by his opponents of failing to appreciate the newness brought about due to the work of Christ. For Calvin, the covenant made with Abraham is the same covenant "in substance and reality" as God has made with his church, only differing in "mode of dispensation."[11] This continuity applies to the old- and new-covenant sacraments as well. The point here is that

9. As a side note, this verse is the key biblical citation used by the Heidelberg Catechism to connect circumcision and baptism when it asks in q. 74, "Should infants be baptized?" and answers "yes."

10. Dennis Johnson, "Infant Baptism: How My Mind Changed," *Reformed Perspectives Magazine* 3 (June 17, 2001) para. 14 (https://thirdmill.org/magazine/article.asp/link/den_johnson%5ETH.Johnson.Baptism.html/at/Infant%20Baptism:%20How%20My%20Mind%20Has%20Changed).

11. Peter Lillback, "Calvin's Interpretation of the History of Salvation," in David W. Hall and Peter A. Lillback, eds., *A Theological Guide to Calvin's Institutes: Essays and Analysis* (Phillipsburg, NJ: P&R, 2008), 168–70.

accepting Calvin's argument in the "Brief Instruction" requires a heavy lift to ascend to a theological framework relating to the Old and New Testaments, and subsequently to circumcision and baptism, that is by no means obvious and is in fact somewhat unique to an eccentricity of Calvin's thought. Those not already convinced of infant baptism could—and do— quite easily construct a different theological framework relating the old and new covenants and circumcision and baptism leading to a different ritual conclusion on infant baptism.

The primary weakness of Calvin's argument—and this will be the primary weakness of the Anabaptist/Baptist counter-argument—is methodological: Calvin seeks to frame the issue as a biblical one. While he notes in passing the historical precedent of infant baptism—namely, that it was practiced before the "papal church" began to exist—he makes clear, "I do not ask antiquity to legitimate anything for us unless it is founded on the Word of God. . . . Let us come, therefore, to the true rule of God . . . that is to say, His Word, which *alone* ought to hold here."[12] But Scripture says nothing explicit about baptizing infants and hardly anything connecting circumcision and baptism. The most Calvin's argument does is demonstrate a level of consonance between infant baptism and Scripture, that infant baptism is not an overt affront to or jarring departure from the biblical witness. But he has not proved, nor can he prove from Scripture, that infant baptism *should* be a normative practice. Calvin arranges scriptural passages, makes theological connections, and draws out conclusions in such a way to justify infant baptism. But those who reject infant baptism are also able to do the same—namely, arrange scriptural passages, make theological connections, and draw out conclusions to reject infant baptism.

Here I'll draw on my own journey once again to illustrate the point. At Beeson Divinity School, during the time when I denied the validity of infant baptism, I took exegetical classes on almost every book of the Bible, some even under infant-baptizing Presbyterians (!), and at no time did I feel challenged to accept infant baptism. I saw it nowhere. Yet when I came to accept the practice as valid, I could then see numerous biblical passages resonating with the practice. So it seems on the topic of infant baptism, Scripture is simply unclear. Both sides of the debate are able to arrange and interpret passages in such a way to defend their side.

It's worth noting that even when the historical record shows that infant baptism had been widely accepted as valid, we still find Christians

12. Calvin, "Brief Instruction," in *Treatises*, 45.

postponing baptism until later in life due to various theological reasons. Tertullian in his *Homily on Baptism*, for example, rejects infant baptism not because it's invalid or contrary to Jesus's or the apostles' teaching or church tradition but based on his unique understanding of the "profitability" of baptism, in which fear and anxiety of post-baptismal moral lapses played a substantial role.[13] The point here is that while everyone accepted the need to be baptized as a normative Christian practice—Scripture was clear on this point—not everyone felt beholden to infant baptism, demonstrating, I believe, the lack of clear biblical witness to the practice. If Scripture were clear on the issue, someone like Tertullian would have never rejected it.

Thus, Anabaptist Balthasar Hubmaier was justified when he rejected infant baptism based on the premise that it was not clearly revealed in Scripture. When asked about infants, Hubmaier responded that he would plead and hope that God would be merciful to them. But *without a clear directive from the Bible*, he concluded that there is nothing more to do than to commit the infants to the Father's hands and ask that His will be done.[14] Baptizing them, however, was not an option.

But herein lies the whole problem of either Calvin's or Hubmaier's arguments—namely, that they conceive of the debate as a biblical argument. Scripture alone will not settle the issue.[15] The work of David Wright is instructive, who, after surveying all the pertinent evidence surrounding the issue of infant baptism in the New Testament and in the incipient church, concludes, "This review has yielded regrettably few certainties."[16] Wright notes that for the first century of the church, there is no evidence to support the claim that infant baptism was a normative practice, nor is there evidence to support it wasn't. The early record is silent on the issue.

And so we come to the key question I was faced with: as a Baptist long nurtured in the Baptist tradition—and this fact is important, for to

13. Ernest Evens trans. and ed., *Tertullian's Homily on Baptism* (London: SPCK, 1964).

14. David C. Steinmetz, "The Baptism of John and the Baptism of Jesus in Huldrych Zwingli, Balthasar Hubmaier and Late Medieval Theology," in *Continuity and Discontinuity in Church History* (Leiden: Brill, 1979), 174.

15. I am aware that my Baptist brethren may dispute this point, claiming Scripture is perfectly clear that only those professing faith for themselves should be baptized. The challenge for them, however, is how to explain the misinterpretation of these passages throughout the history of Christianity starting clearly as early as (though possibly earlier) the second century, with the Baptist interpretation only surfacing at the time of the Reformation.]

16. David F. Wright, *Infant Baptism in Historical Perspective: Collected Studies* (Colorado Springs: Paternoster, 2007), 20.

depart from one's tradition and insert oneself into another is, or should be, a profound and somewhat painful spiritual journey—how did I justify breaking from my tradition with regard to a practice that does not receive explicit support in Scripture and can at best be ambiguously reconcilable with Scripture and may not have been a widespread practice in early apostolic times as far as we can tell?

Barth and Church Tradition

At this point, I want to bring in Karl Barth to help put the issue of affirming or denying infant baptism in stark relief. Barth denied the validity of infant baptism. While he was mistaken in claiming that only in the Constantinian revolution of the fourth century did infant baptism become a general rule and that "there is a genuine doctrine of infant baptism only from the time of the Reformation," he hits on something important when he observes, "The presupposition of the [Reformers'] proofs of the practice was a recognition of the validity of the powerful fact of church history whereby infant baptism had long since become the rule in Christendom. Even the churches of the Reformation thought they must yield to the fact of church history and accept its claim to validity."[17] It is church history—or we might say Christian *tradition*, and how we understand and apply that tradition in relation to Scripture—that is the foundation upon which affirming infant baptism stands or falls. For Barth, it falls, for he judges that the Reformers justified "something alien, a foreign body, which they were not prepared to reject, and which, for good or evil, they thus had to live with, trying to assimilate it into the rest of their teaching."[18] I, however, came to the opposite conclusion on infant baptism for the very reason Barth rejects it.

Infant baptism reveals acutely how Christianity is not just a set of ideas about God, man, salvation, and such; but it is more fully a way of being human in the world, intellectually, morally, and ritually. Participating in the rite of baptism has always characterized the way of being Christian in the world, even if the theology of baptism has not always been crystal clear. And we know that infant participation in the rite of baptism has characterized the way of being Christian from at least the second century (and possibly even earlier—again, the evidence is inconclusive), even if the theological explanation for infant baptism has been variously understood.

17. Karl Barth, *Church Dogmatics* IV/4 (Edinburgh: T&T Clark, 1961), 162.
18. Barth, *Church Dogmatics* IV/4, 162.

As Wright comments, "If there is a persistent controversy about infant baptism in the patristic age, it concerns primarily the question of 'why?' rather than 'whether?,' although the absence of confident answers to the former must have to some extent diverted pressure onto the latter."[19]

When Anabaptists and Baptists reject infant baptism, they do so by extracting themselves from participation in the stream of Christianity—the tradition—flowing from its origins and instead, now unbeholden to that stream, rearrange the pieces of the biblical puzzle to reach an unprecedented theological conclusion that runs counter to the historical ritual embodiment of the Christian faith. They have no more substantial ground to stand on than their particular interpretive arrangement of Scripture—which, as I've argued, can simply be countered with a different interpretive approach to Scripture that supports infant baptism, as Calvin did (and had been done for the almost entirety of Christianity before the sixteenth century). The Anabaptists were not reading anything in Scripture that the church hadn't been reading for centuries already, and it's not as if scriptural passages explicitly affirming infant baptism had suddenly vanished. So in the end what changed was not what the Bible said or didn't say about baptism but how those rejecting infant baptism read Scripture. Scripture was now read in isolation from its reception in the lived beliefs and practices of God's people. Calvin's argument was no different. While concluding in favor of infant baptism, he framed the issue as a strictly biblical argument. He, too, treated the meaning of Scripture as accessible apart from its reception in the tradition as a hermeneutical guide for its proper interpretation and embodiment. Therein lies the crux of the issue.

The Development of the Doctrine of the Trinity as a Parallel Example

My arguments here on infant baptism have a parallel in the development of the doctrine of the Trinity in the Nicene-Constantinopolitan era.[20] As Lewis Ayers's and Khaled Anatolios's work on the historical development

19. Wright, *Infant Baptism*, 29.

20. It has long been a curiosity to me how Baptists can affirm the doctrine of the Trinity according to the Nicene-Constantinopolitan framework but reject infant baptism. Neither are explicitly affirmed in Scripture in the way they would be in the church's reception of Scripture (i.e., the Tradition). Yet one is affirmed while the other is denied, supposedly based on "what Scripture says."

of Trinity has made clear, debates in the fourth and fifth centuries about God's triune existence were not just philosophical and theological but also deeply exegetical. As Anatolios states of the competing factions, "There was general agreement on the contents of the scriptural canon, its normativity as the prime source of divine revelation, and the attribution of its ultimate authorship to the Holy Spirit. Thus, all parties in the trinitarian conflicts constructed their arguments in scriptural terms, without any disagreements on canonicity."[21] Much like with infant baptism, passages could be cited and arranged and interpreted in such a way to support different sides of the debate.

Thus at some level, embracing the Nicene-Constantinopolitan understanding of God and Christ requires believing that the Spirit guided the Councils of Nicaea and Constantinople to establish the proper hermeneutical framework for understanding Scripture; it is a reliance on the church to establish proper biblical interpretation. Claiming to accept Nicaea as true simply on the basis that it rightly interprets Scripture only begs the question that plagued the time of Nicaea, which was, again, the proper interpretive framework for understanding Scripture. At its heart, to affirm God and Christ as explained according to the Nicene-Constantinopolitan Councils is to make a judgment about history—that is, about tradition.

It should come as no surprise that the same methodological impetus to reject infant baptism, namely by extracting Scripture from its lived interpretive experience within the church, opened the radical Reformers to rejecting other "traditional" doctrines like Nicene Trinitarianism. As Ulrich Lehner puts it in his description of the unitarian Faustus Socini (1539–1604), "Socinus' Christianity . . . was founded upon a strict Biblicism that lacked any regulative principle except the principle of noncontradiction."[22] As the fourth- and fifth-century debates on the Trinity demonstrated, the Bible is sufficiently unclear in and of itself, extracted from the larger hermeneutical framework that includes the lived worship and practice of the church, on the exact framework for understanding the proper relationship of Father, Son, and Holy Spirit that different conclusions based on appeals to different

21. Khaled Anatolios, *Retrieving Nicaea: The Development and Meaning of Trinitarian Doctrine* (Grand Rapids: Baker Academic, 2011), 36; see also Lewis Ayres, *Nicaea and Its Legacy: An Approach to Fourth-Century Trinitarian Theology* (New York: Oxford University Press, 2004).

22. Ulrich L. Lehner, "The Trinity in the Early Modern Era (c. 1550–1770)," in Gilles Emery and Matthew Levering, eds., *Oxford Handbook on the Trinity* (New York: Oxford University Press, 2014), 245.

Scriptures could be drawn, just as with the case of infant baptism. Thus, a narrow appeal to Scripture alone among the radical Reformers—that is, their intentional dismissal of the church's tradition as the context for proper biblical exegesis—was able to lead to both the rejection of infant baptism and the rejection of Nicene Trinitarianism.

Moreover, whether it's Anatolios's understanding of primary and secondary reflection or Bernard Lonergan's use of undifferentiated and differentiated consciousness to explain doctrinal development,[23] all agree that once a doctrine has been established, a change necessarily occurs in how one subjectively approaches the object of the doctrine. While there is certainly continuity between how God and Christ were understood by Christians of the first century and Christians after Nicaea, there is also a change that necessarily occurred in one's approach to God and Christ due to the doctrinal constructions of Nicaea and the concepts, clarity, and general patterns of reasoning that became part of the experience of worship due to Nicaea. Said another way, to participate in confessing God as triune according to Nicaea is therefore to be not biblical, in the strict sense of the term, but rather to be a person of both Scripture and tradition as a unified deposit of Christian truth.

Baptists who have and continue to affirm Nicene Trinitarianism—which is the vast majority of them, as evidenced whether by the early 1689 Baptist confession of faith known as the Second London Confession, or the recent 2020 Baptist Faith and Message—but reject infant baptism are being selective and somewhat arbitrary in picking through the very same tradition that bequeathed both infant baptism and Nicene Trinitarianism. The tradition, which handed down Nicene Trinitarianism as the proper hermeneutical and doctrinal framework for worshipping the God and Christ of Scripture, also handed down the practice of infant baptism as a proper liturgical practice of biblical Christianity. To appeal to the Bible to reject infant baptism is to beg the question of proper biblical interpretation, just as with Nicene Trinitarianism. The tradition has spoken on both, and it says that the God of our worship is triune, and the practice of infant baptism is a valid liturgical practice. Neither are unbiblical, even if neither are explicitly stated in Scripture.

23. Bernard Lonergan, *The Way to Nicea* (Philadelphia: Westminster, 1976).

Conclusion: The Real Break

When it came to accepting infant baptism as a valid sacramental practice, I discovered that what really marked the beginnings of my departure with my Baptist tradition was my approach to church history—that is, to the tradition. I had been formed by my Baptist context not just to root my beliefs about the Christian faith in Scripture but also in some sense to confine my beliefs to Scripture. What mattered was today and the biblical day. The intervening centuries varied in the degrees of relevance in determining how I interpreted the Bible and what beliefs and practices I believed should be accepted by the church.

What I discovered in my journey through my two master's degrees and PhD in theology is that I began as a Baptist simply learning about church history as mere "facts" to be studied. At some point the church's history morphed into a living, breathing, and speaking tradition to be resourced for present faith and practice. Eventually, this living tradition would become determinative—authoritative—for how I approached Scripture and embodied the Christian faith. And thus for me, when it came to infant baptism, I was faced with a practice almost universally accepted since, without a doubt, the second century, and possibly earlier. And even with the reevaluation of the Christian faith that occurred during the Reformation, it was a practice that was accepted by all Reformation traditions except a very small minority.

In addition, with no biblical prohibition against infant baptism in Scripture, with general agreement between biblical principles and infant baptism, with reasonable explanations as to why most people recorded being baptized in Scripture were adults (i.e., these were the first converts, so naturally they would be adults), with the precedent of circumcision as a rite of inclusion of infants, and with my Baptist brethren feeling so compelled to do something with infants of believing parents that they perform the practice of baby dedication, I felt compelled to submit to the living Christian faith as it had been embodied and passed on to me with regard to infant baptism. And this is ultimately *why* I changed my mind on infant baptism.

www.ingramcontent.com/pod-product-compliance
Lightning Source LLC
Chambersburg PA
CBHW030849090426
42737CB00009B/1165

Published by K. Sawa Marketing International Inc. DBA Jumpstart Publishing. PO Box 6, Roseville, CA 95661. (916) 872-4000 JumpstartPublishing.net

DISCLAIMER AND/OR LEGAL NOTICES

ISBN: 979-8-218-26689-9

PRINTED IN THE UNITED STATES

PARENTING MARATHON

THE 10-STEP GUIDE TO NAVIGATE PARENTING CHALLENGES

By **Dana Parisi**

CEO and Founder of
LivesTouchedCoaching.com

LIVES
TOUCHED
PARENT COACHING AND
FAMILY WELLNESS

Dedication

This book is dedicated to my amazing family: to my husband who has been my partner and journeyed on many Parenting Marathons with me, and to my four children who I am incredibly proud of. In the chapters ahead, I share some of our stories and struggles, but I could write several books about the ways they each have amazed me with their growth, compassion, empathy, and courage. Kids, I love you forever and ever and always.

Table of Contents

Introduction:
YOU HAVE ENTERED A PARENTING MARATHON

Have you ever *accidentally* signed up to run a marathon?

Probably not.

If you sign up for a marathon, chances are good that you know, at least in part, what you're getting into.

Have you accidentally signed up for a Parenting Marathon?

Now *that* is entirely possible.

While approximately one percent of the population will participate in a running marathon, 100% of parents will experience a Parenting Marathon. Of course we're all aware, when we become parents, that there will be challenges along the way. Whether we enter our parenting journey through the birth of biological children, adoption, foster care, guardianship, or gain step-children through marriage, we know there will be highs and lows. But really, how much can we know in advance? We may have vague ideas of the challenges and an abundance of confidence in our abilities, we may feel uncertain and fearful from the start, or anything in between. Expected or unexpected, challenges are going to come and when they do... we discover that we are signed up for a Parenting Marathon!

So, what is a Parenting Marathon?

A Parenting Marathon is a challenging and prolonged season of parenting that requires perseverance, strength, perspective, and skills. It is also an **opportunity** for growth in yourself and your family.

Since a running marathon is 26.2 miles, let's consider any parenting challenge that lasts more than 26 days to be a Parenting Marathon. There are shorter seasons of challenges to be sure, but if the challenging situation you are in lasts 26 days or more, you are in an endurance event! This book is for you.

There are many varieties of Parenting Marathons, and you are likely to encounter at least one during your parenting years. Some examples of possible Parenting Marathons:

- a newborn baby who seems to cry non-stop and nothing comforts him

- a toddler who is "strong-willed" and wants to rule the roost

- a middle schooler struggling to navigate their place in the world

- a teenager struggling with depression or anxiety

- a foster or adopted child who has experienced loss and trauma and now acts out in bizarre and confusing ways

- a step-child who seems to reject a step-parent

- a childhood medical diagnosis

- a neurodiverse child (ADHD or Autism Spectrum) who's struggling at home and school

- siblings who seem to be always fighting

- grandparents who become parents of their grandchildren

- a child/teen or young adult who's making risky choices

- sandwich generation parents who are parenting their kids and also providing significant support to their aging parents

- being a source of support for adult children managing life's various challenges

This is just a sampling of the races you may be in the middle of.

I wish that I could sit down with you, just the two of us, and hear your story. What does your current Parenting Marathon look like? What made you pick up this book? How are you holding up in this endurance event of life? How much energy do you have left? Each one of us has a story. They are each unique, but as parents of kids in tough seasons, we have many things in common. There is hope and growth waiting for all of us.

Maybe you are feeling exhausted, like everything you try falls flat. It might feel like you are unable to affect a positive outcome no matter what you do. Maybe you're feeling isolated and alone in the journey. It might be hard to remember the feeling of joy in your parenting. Perhaps you are plagued by fear and anxiety? Maybe parenting is not looking at all like you pictured it.

You are not alone.

During the 17 years I've been a mom, I have run and completed many Parenting Marathons. So many that I've wondered, "Why me? Am I doing something wrong? I didn't realize exactly what I signed up for!" My four children (two biological and two adopted) have each brought unique, and often confusing, Parenting Marathons. My husband and I experienced two preterm births with weeks of hospitalizations. As parents, we've seen many challenges in our kids including sensory processing disorders, ADHD, Obsessive Compulsive symptoms, anxiety, depression, and adoption related issues including: early life trauma, loss, attachment trauma, lying, stealing, rages, defiance, aggression, and learning difficulties.

It was during one of my toughest Parenting Marathons that I started dreaming about being a source of support for other parents. In 2021, I became a Certified Parent Coach and am blessed to work with parents virtually throughout the country. The more I talk honestly with other parents about the Parenting Marathons I've been through or am currently in, the more I hear about other parents' stories. Parents have shared their stories of kids who are struggling with suicidal thoughts, sexual identity, depression, breaking laws, eating disorders, social anxiety, addictions, neurodiversity, panic attacks, rejection and more. We can't exactly walk in each other's shoes, but we can relate and support one another. The support I've received over the years has been invaluable to me. No parent should have to feel alone or hopeless.

Through years of "lacing up my Parenting Marathon shoes," I became exhausted and was losing my sense of joy. I found myself going through the motions, with the main goal of getting through the next stretch of time. Get through the day... or just the morning, or maybe just one meal at a time. If you have a child who is struggling, the parenting role can quickly become much tougher than you expected. Our kids' struggles come in different packages, but regardless of the specific details, they universally take a toll on the caregivers who are trying to guide them toward healthy futures.

Journeying with kids who are struggling is a marathon, and running a marathon requires:

- multiple incremental steps
- time
- perseverance
- support

There is no way around it, a Parenting Marathon is tough. And, there is also joy waiting to be found in the journey! Throughout this book, I hope you will discover your strength and joy. I know you will find that *you* are tougher than you expected!

My goal for you is that you take away 2-3 of these training tools and start to implement them this week. Use this book as a reference and come back to review these steps with the new parenting challenges you encounter (there's a "quick glance" section after each step to make it easy for you). Remember this book is here for you. Please save it in a safe place, almost like you might keep on speed dial a trusted friend!

The Starting Line

A running marathon is not something that everyone is interested in. Those who decide to take on the 26.2 miles know that they need to **prepare**. I personally used to hate running. Upon moving to Eau Claire, Wisconsin, where running is a popular activity, I often was asked, "Are you a runner?" "Only If I'm chasing down one of my kids," I would reply. Seriously, many people here are dedicated to running. It's common to see people running in snowstorms, bundled up to their eyes and trudging through biting winter winds. "Who does that?" I would ask out loud, as I drove my minivan full of kids home.

But as we know, life takes its twists and turns and I found myself, years later, in a season where I needed something different. I wasn't exactly sure what I needed, but I knew I needed something. My family had recently grown again. We had welcomed our fourth child home. This was our family's second adoption, and our new son was two and a half years old. It was a season of celebrating his home-coming, and it also ushered in a season of changes. Helping our youngest son adjust to a new home, new family, new country, new language, new everything, was only one small part of the season. Now, parenting four kids, I was more stretched and stressed than ever before. It felt like parenting each of my kids could be considered a full-time job in itself. My husband's job had him working during almost all of the kids' waking hours. I was maxed out. Our third child, who was also adopted when she was two years old and was now in first grade, started having more struggles. She was struggling to keep up at school, but the harder part was that her challenging behaviors at home were seriously ramping up. I was running a Parenting Marathon and didn't realize it yet.

Fast forward a bit into that season, and I, a non-runner, joined a women's running group. I didn't join because I liked running or because I thought I'd be good at it. I joined because I needed other active women in my life. I knew I needed something, and fresh air and movement seemed like a good place to start. As I ran more, I grew to love it. Running meant time for me to breathe, take care of myself, get outside, be quiet if I wanted to, or talk with friends. It became a lifeline in a difficult parenting season.

By my second year as a runner, I had participated in three half marathons and I decided to train for a full marathon. The things that I learned in my training turned out to be skills I needed for my Parenting Marathons, as well.

The following are 10 essential training steps for a (running or parenting) marathon:

1. Define your goals

2. Take care of yourself on the journey

3. Have a plan, but be willing to be flexible

4. Keep track and watch for progress and patterns

5. Simplify

6. Get support

7. Focus on the positives, look for joy in the journey

8. Avoid comparison

9. Don't wallow in guilt over failures

10. Step up to the starting line

Parenting Marathons are a lot like training for a running marathon. We want to raise our kids to be joyful and successful. We know it's going to take endurance, patience, and skill to reach that goal. There will be challenges, setbacks, and frustrations, but also victories and joy. We could use a Parenting Marathon "training plan," don't you think? Great! Because that is what this book is! Enjoy and please reach out to me with your comments and thoughts as you're going through the book.

At the end of every chapter, including this introduction, is a section labeled "Your Turn." You'll get the most out of this book if you take a few minutes and reflect on the questions. What I've also done to make it easy for you, is put all of the journaling exercises, as well as some additional tips and resources in a handy downloadable workbook that you can get access to for free on my website. The page to get your workbook, a bonus free training video, extra resources to support you, and to reach out to me with your comments and thoughts is www.ParentingMarathon.com/resources.

Your Turn:

1. What Parenting Marathons have you experienced so far on your parenting journey? List them here.

2. What does your current Parenting Marathon look like? Describe it below.

"Be practical as well as generous in your ideals. Keep your eyes on the stars but remember to keep your feet on the ground."

- THEODORE ROOSEVELT

Step One:

DEFINE YOUR GOALS

Are you typically a goal setter? We all have some experience with setting good intentions (maybe around New Year) and then falling short of the goal. Don't worry if you don't have a perfect track record with your past goals. These will be goals you can succeed with!

After signing up for my first marathon, a running friend with far more experience than myself asked me what my goal was for the race. I was hesitant to put a time goal on myself without any prior marathon experience, so I told her my goal was "to finish it." We talked about possible time goals that might be reasonable, and I really didn't know what to say. To me, it wasn't about how fast I could go. She asked me what was motivating me to run a marathon. My motivation... That took more consideration. I realized that a big part of my motivation was to stay engaged with running outside throughout the long Wisconsin winter (yup, I had become one of the crazies running in snowstorms). Her comment stuck with me. She said, "by the time the marathon morning arrives you will have already accomplished your goal!"

The goal isn't just a finish line, the goal is also the journey.

As I mentioned in the introduction, each time you find yourself in a Parenting Marathon, you might want to return to this chapter to define your goals for that situation. Right now, think about the one you're currently in.

Do you have goals for the Parenting Marathon you're in? Even if you've never written down a parenting goal, I bet that you have some in your head. Our goals are often linked to the values we prioritize, the ideals that we feel are the most important. This is true in all sorts of areas: parenting, work, and how we use our free time. If you value independence, you might prioritize teaching your kids skills that will help them be more independent, like doing their own laundry and cooking. If you value making a difference in the lives of others, you likely model generosity, and encourage your kids to find ways to volunteer and serve others.

When I was setting my first marathon goals, the question about my motivation was really a glimpse into some of my values. Since I value physical and mental health, I focused my goals on the process of training over how fast I ran the race. Another runner might focus on getting their best time, running with and supporting a friend, or the adventure of seeing new places. Don't judge your values as good or bad, rather use them to understand what's motivating *you*.

Understanding what your values are in your current Parenting Marathon will help you keep perspective on the big picture, and decide how you want to respond to various situations. For example, if you have a child who has missing school assignments, your values will play a role in determining how you respond. A high value on performance and grades might cause you to remind, beg, or bribe your child into getting their work done. If you value personal growth, you might see this as an opportunity for your child to learn from their mistakes, and decide to stay less involved.

It can be stressful when there is a disconnect between our values and the priorities, decisions, or behaviors of our child. Think about the things that your kids do (or don't do) that drive you crazy. I love a clean and organized home, and value simplicity, so it's not surprising that it's like fingernails on a chalkboard when I see my kids' rooms looking like a war zone. At the same time, connecting with my kids and building a strong relationship is more important. I know from experience that nagging them every day about their rooms will make all of us resentful. So now I chose to ignore the rooms until Saturday rolls around, which is family cleaning day. Closing the bedroom doors helps me keep my cool the rest of the week.

Our values are going to affect our parenting goals, and we also need to consider the fact that in parenting, there are things we can control and things we can't. Our Parenting Marathon goals should focus on the things we *can* control, like how we show up, grow through the challenges, are intentional, and model persistence and unconditional love. Perhaps you have a large end goal, a "finish line" you want to cross in this Parenting Marathon. Don't define yourself strictly by the outcome though. Recognize that going through the journey day by day *is* reaching your goal. Every time you show up and put love and energy into navigating this season with your child, you are accomplishing the goal.

During my work as a parent coach, I love to help parents define their goals. Let me introduce you to Sally, a mom of a child who experienced early life trauma. When we started working together, she told me that she felt like she was not a "good mom." I asked why she felt that way and she said, "because my daughter misbehaves and doesn't listen." In our time working together, I wanted her to see that defining her success as a "good mom" based solely on her daughter's behavior was a dangerous trap. Of course, as parents, we want to positively influence our kids' behavior and choices, but we can't make all of their choices for them. You may teach your child not to call other people names, not to get into fights, cheat on tests, or argue with teachers, but he/she may still choose to do it. I encouraged her to look at what she does have control over. Although her child was making choices that resulted in getting into trouble at school and frustrating her parents, this mom did have control over many things.

Sally *did* have control over choosing to be on a learning journey. She learned to be more mindful and intentional of how she responded to her daughter's challenging behaviors. She learned ways to continue to teach and model their family values and appropriate interactions. Her daughter had intense needs for reassurance and security, and Sally learned to make adjustments in their schedules and daily lives to meet her needs. With guidance, she learned she could nurture the good in her child while also correcting and redirecting the negative behavior. Ultimately, she recognized that she *is* a "good mom," and she was showing up for her child every day. It feels much less hopeless when our goals are reachable by our own actions, and not by the choices of others.

Consider if you had the following goal in mind: "My high-schooler will get into an Ivy League University." You could jump through every hoop, take your teen to every college visit, pay for test prep courses to help her be prepared and sit with her while she does her applications. But what if she doesn't get in, chooses a different college or takes a gap year? These aren't signs of failure in your Parenting Marathon. Perhaps redefining the goal is what's needed. Perhaps your goal could be "I will support my high-schooler as she chooses her options for after high-school." That is a goal YOU have control over!

What if you really, really want (and need) your toddler to sleep through the night in his own bed. A goal of "Billy will sleep in his own bed throughout the night" sounds lovely, but every sleep-deprived parent knows we can't make our kids sleep. Redefining the goal might look like "I will set up a peaceful evening routine to help Billy feel calm, safe and relaxed at bedtime." This is something you have control over. The outcome will likely be better sleep for everyone, but the goal is focused on the journey, not merely the finish line.

A parent of a child who has regular meltdowns or rages definitely wants to see more peace and calm in the home. A great goal might be "I will learn more tools to stay calm and help my child calm down when he's out of control. I will look at what the behavior is communicating to me and what might be triggering it." These goals are within your grasp as a parent! It's a lot harder to reach a goal such as: "My child won't get mad when he's asked to do a chore." Make goals for what YOU have control over, and you will see the benefits in your child.

Here are some other examples of possible goals:

> "My goal is to rediscover joy in my parenting journey."

> "My goal is to invest time each week into enjoying my child's company in order to maintain (or get back to) a positive relationship."

> "My goal is to not define myself by my child's success or struggles."

> "My goal is to bounce back quicker after my child and I have a rough moment."

> "My goal is to nurture my child's strengths and help him explore his interests."

Your Turn:

1. Write down 1-2 of your goals for your current Parenting Marathon.

Step One Quick Glance:

When you're setting goals for your Parenting Marathon, consider:

- Your motivation and values
- What you have control over
- Looking at the journey, not only at the finish line

"Almost everything will work again if you unplug it for a few minutes, including you."

- ANNE LAMOTT

Step Two:

TAKE CARE OF YOURSELF ON THE JOURNEY

How do you feel about the words "self-care"? Many parents I talk with sort of laugh or shrug. For busy, stressed parents, there's often a dual sense that we **know** we need self-care, but how exactly are we supposed to make it happen? It might even start to feel like one more thing on the "to-do" list.

- Make dinner

- Do thc laundry

- Get kids to sports

- And so on, and so on...

- Oh ya, don't forget self-care

While training for a running marathon, I thought about self-care in terms of getting enough sleep, eating healthy foods, drinking plenty of water, stretching tired muscles, and maybe even getting a massage once in a while. It made sense to me that in order to keep increasing the training miles and intensity, I would need to take care of myself. But taking time for self-care was much harder for me to accept when it came to my Parenting Marathons.

We may know in our heads that we need to take care of ourselves, but when you're in a state of exhaustion from your Parenting Marathon, it may feel like you can't even catch your breath. What exactly is self-care? When are you supposed to find the time? Does self-care mean a manicure or massage, and how's that going to help anyways?

You know that dealing with struggling kids taxes your personal resources of energy, time, patience, compassion, and empathy. You also probably sense, maybe deep down, that you can't keep going at this rate forever. Perhaps you feel like you are starting to unravel? I certainly have felt that unraveling during my toughest moments. It was at my lowest point in a Parenting Marathon, when I felt the most hopeless and discouraged, that I finally got serious about self-care.

Our family consists of four kids, my husband, and myself. We have two biological and two adopted children. All children, regardless of how they join a family, will go through various struggles as they grow and each of their stories are unique. Part of our adoption journeys included wrapping our minds around the early life losses that our kids experienced. There can be various traumas in a child's life prior to their adoption, and those traumas have an impact.

In this "unraveling" season of my parenting, we were seeing significant stress, dysregulation, anger, and aggression in our daughter who joined our family through international adoption. It seemed like anything could set off a new epic meltdown. I felt like I was constantly walking through a minefield hoping not to trigger an explosion, but knowing that it would inevitably happen. There were multiple rages a day that I would swear "came out of nowhere." I was getting screamed at, pinched, pushed, and worn down. Confusingly, she would be simultaneously trying to hurt me while also trying to climb into my lap to be comforted. We were dealing with the effects of attachment trauma caused by earlier losses in her life. Everyday felt like survival mode for me as a parent.

At the time, I sort of understood that the baffling behaviors were signs of my daughter's stress, but it felt like they were aimed at making me miserable. I desperately wanted to help her but felt like nothing was working. If I could have paid for some sort of magic wand to "fix" things, I would have probably paid any price. I was in a steep uphill stretch of this Parenting Marathon, and there was no end in sight.

In a running marathon, it doesn't necessarily start out feeling terribly hard. The early miles might feel very manageable. But the miles keep piling up... maybe there are hills to climb, bad weather, a blister or a pain that interferes... and at some point, you realize that this is just plain rough. The same can be true for Parenting Marathons. You may not realize that it's getting hard at first, or that your energy is waning.

In this particular Parenting Marathon, there were a number of contributing factors that got us to the crisis point we were at. My daughter struggled in first grade with learning and an undiagnosed vision problem.

She must have felt frustrated and stressed daily while at school, but didn't feel comfortable asking for help. By the middle of first grade, she was feeling desperate enough that she pleaded with me to homeschool her for second grade. I was reluctant, because at home, most requests or challenges were met with big emotions. I could only imagine the extra burden being in charge of her education would put on us. My daughter is also incredibly social, and I knew she would miss her classmates if we changed to homeschooling.

I held off making a decision, thinking this idea would pass. Over the second half of her first-grade year, she continued to plead with me to work with her at home for second grade. I was skeptical but eventually relented when I was lucky enough to get a deeper glimpse into how she was feeling. The discussion of homeschool came up for the umpteenth time, and I finally said to her, "I just don't understand why you want to be homeschooled for the year." In the past, she hadn't been able to put it into words and would simply say "I just want to." This time she said, "I don't understand what they're teaching me, and they just keep giving me more and more work, and it's over-flooding me." Over-flooding... that was the word that did it.

I didn't want her to feel like she was drowning in school. She was attending a Montessori School at the time and her class was composed of first, second, and third graders. She was the kind of student who didn't make waves or cause trouble at school. She listened to directions, was sweet and compliant to teachers, and appeared busy during work time. When she didn't understand the assignment or project, she

24

would quietly shove it in her backpack rather than ask for an explanation. Then she would pretend to be busy with something else so as not to draw negative attention to herself. I knew she was falling through the cracks at her school, and with a one-on-one personalized approach in homeschool, I could make sure she understood the lesson before we moved on. The longer I let the idea sit with me, the more I started getting excited about homeschooling. We would have the opportunity to build our relationship and connect more, and I would have the chance to help her love learning. I was excited, but I wasn't really prepared for how hard it would be.

After the first two months of trying everything I could think of to connect, make learning fun, and still help her make progress, I was exhausted, discouraged and frankly, I was falling apart. Each day, I woke up early to prepare and pray for the day. Each morning, I put my feet to the floor once again and was determined to make the day successful. But even though my mind said "you can keep going," my body was rebelling. I felt chronically stressed, and was sleeping poorly. My migraine headaches doubled. I started developing heart palpitations. Two weeks into my heart's new bizarre rhythm, I woke with a cold sore on my lip and an irritated puffy stye on my eyelid. Are you getting the ugly picture? My body was responding to the stress my mind was trying to overlook. I felt like giving up. Sadly, my most desperate thought during that season was, "I wish I could escape."

The behaviors I was dealing with at home were exhausting me and affecting every area of my life. My relationships with my other three kids were suffering, as well as my relationship with my husband who didn't often see the same struggles when he was home. I lacked the margin in my life to invest in my adult friendships. Physically and mentally, I was struggling.

I was experiencing parental burnout. Feeling like giving up, but knowing that wasn't an option, I was desperate to find better solutions. As with any journey, I had to start somewhere. Self-care was an important starting point. It was also necessary for maintenance; maintenance of my energy, perseverance and compassion. If you're in a Parenting Marathon, self-care is a must. You've probably heard the phrase "self-care isn't selfish," which is absolutely true, but I will tell you that it's also *crucial* to your success.

So where can you start when it comes to self-care for your Parenting Marathon? Start small. I took some advice from a wise woman, and put pen to paper. I wrote out 20 things I would enjoy doing if I had 10 minutes of free time. My list included: read a book, organize family photos into a digital album, sit on the porch, pet the cat, stretch, call a friend, have a cup of tea, pray, do a sudoku puzzle on the iPad, listen to music. Then I wrote down 20 things I would enjoy doing if I had an hour of free time, and 3-6 hours of free time. This may seem like a trivial starting point, but it put me back in the mind frame of being intentional about self-care. It wasn't easy for me to think of things for my list. I was so used to multi-tasking and using all my time and energy for my family and their various needs. I also wasn't good at asking for or accepting help, but I started leaning into my support system (more on that later). Every day I planned to be intentional and do at least two things from my "10 minute" list. Spoiler alert: you are going to start your list soon.

First, let's cover three elements of self-care:

1. The 3 Pauses technique for daily recharging

2. Recharge Retreat

3. Sleep

3 Pauses Technique for Daily Recharging

We joke in my family that at 10:00 p.m., our golden retriever Thor goes "off duty." Normally, Thor can't get enough attention, but when he's off duty, it's clear that he's ready for a break. He heads to his bed, takes a deep sigh, and is done for the day. How about you? Do you ever feel like you are "off duty"? Your answer likely depends on the ages and stages of your kids. As parents, we don't "clock out" or get work breaks built into our days. In just a bit we'll talk about taking a "Recharge Retreat," a break from the work and stress of being a parent. It can be amazing and rejuvenating! However, we can't run our personal energy tanks to empty every day and then hope for a weekend break that will undo the damage to our well-being.

Learning to be proactive each day to find simple ways to recharge will make a huge difference in your energy, outlook, and ability to stay calm in tough moments. 3 Pauses is the simple technique of taking three brief pauses of 5-15 minutes in your day to do something that brings you energy, peace, or joy. As parents, we become in tune with our kids' energy levels and know how important it is to build in ways for them to recharge. I'm sure you've noticed when your child needs a snack, a drink, or a break from the action. 3 Pauses will help *you* be more intentional about keeping your own personal battery charged.

Find out what is restful for you, set a timer for 5-15 minutes, and give yourself the gift of three short pauses a day. Maybe it's listening to music you love, playing an instrument, deep breathing, sitting outside, stretching, reading a devotional or inspirational book, listening to birds, reading, taking a walk, calling a friend, having a cup of tea, singing, writing poetry, drawing or coloring, working on a craft, or playing a game. Try different things, find what works for you, and build it into your day. Be mindful if you find you're tempted to "fill" those pauses with multi-tasking, checking email, returning texts, or doom scrolling social media, which may not leave you feeling recharged.

Since each pause is for such a short period of time, it's very doable to add them into your busy days. Here are some examples of how I and parents that I work with are incorporating pauses into the day:

- Pre-Game: carving out time for a pause before the kids wake up.

- Lunch Break: resisting the urge to multitask while you eat, and instead enjoying your food while you sit and relax.

- Brought my Book: using one of the small chunks of time that you have while you wait for kids at activities.

- Post-Work Transition: taking a few minutes after work and before you reunite with your family.

- Commute: using your drive time for self-care by enjoying silence or listening to something uplifting.

- Prep for Transition: knowing which transitions are typically challenging for your child (like coming home from school or a sports activity), and carving out a little time to take care of yourself beforehand.

- Off Duty: kids are in bed, and even if there is more work to be done in the house, take a pause.

My dad went through surgical residency in the 1970s. The hours and stress were grueling, and those were the days well before the mandatory 40-hour work week limit for residents. A week of 90-plus hours was normal. It turned out that the residents who were smokers had built in breaks in their long days. Smoking was allowed in the hospital in those days, and the smokers took 10-15 minute breaks multiple times a day to smoke. This appeared to be an acceptable reason to pause from the residents' stressful work. But what about the non-smokers? Well, there wasn't an acceptable reason to take a break, so they kept working. Hmmm, does it come as much of a surprise that my dad took up smoking during this period of time in his life? Good news for us, we don't need to pick up an unhealthy habit in order to give ourselves permission to rest! We just need to believe that we are worthy of rest, and build pauses into our days.

Your Turn:

1. Make your list. Write down at least 20 things you would enjoy doing when you take a short pause of 5-15 minutes.

2. Bonus: write down 20 things you would enjoy doing if you have an hour of free time.

If you're like me, you might be tempted to read on and skip making these lists, but don't do it. Be intentional and make your list so you can start adding in self-care. You can also head to the free resource page. There you will find a list of ideas to consider, and you can simply circle the ones you like! www. ParentingMarathon.com/resources

Recharge Retreat

After years of parenting around the clock, I finally hit the promised land... half-day kindergarten! Our youngest child started 4K, or "four-year-old kindergarten." All four of my kids would be out of the house from the glorious hours of 8:00 a.m. to noon! "What will you do with your time off?" I was asked over and over again. If you have been in the season of half-day school, you may relate to the feeling that this time moves at hyper speed. My ambitions for what I would do usually outpaced the reality of that limited time. I certainly got things done: my part-time job, groceries, laundry, house cleaning, running errands, appointments, a little exercise, meal prep, organization for the kids' activities and clubs, some volunteer work... but there should be *some* down time, right?

I hadn't yet discovered the power of the 3 Pauses, and so I found myself spinning my wheels at every opportunity to sit and be still. I just kept "going" instead of recharging my own energy.

My mind would race through things that needed to get done. There was an email I needed to send off, a text I hadn't responded to, preparation for the evening activities I should start, items to add to my next shopping list, one more attempt to pick up the house before it got destroyed again. I struggled to be still. Resentment would build up in me because it seemed like there was a never ending list of things to be done, but no one else seemed as concerned about it as I was. In the evenings, when other people in my family rested or had fun, I was frustrated that there was still more work for *me* to do. I needed to physically leave my house in order to feel rested. Taking a run, or going out with a friend gave me a break from the work I saw everywhere around me at home.

I started exploring what a recharge retreat meant to me. As parents, we are simultaneously learning about our children, and about ourselves. What an incredible thing! Discovering that I recharge by being alone was a game changer for me. I love time with friends and family, and I used to feel guilty that I was worn out after too many human interactions. Discovering more about myself helped me make peace with the fact that as an introvert, time to myself is like plugging in the battery. Alone time gives me the energy, recovery, and perspective I need to rejoin the people I love as my best self. One solution I found that had huge benefits was to start being proactive with scheduling a "mom-cation."

*Mom-cation: A vacation from the daily work and stress of being a mom.
(also known as a parent-cation or dad-cation)

Sure... but how? In order to schedule a mom-cation I needed to ask for help. It's not easy for many of us parents to ask for help. We're used to being the ones to help others. Asking for and accepting help is hard, but it's worth it. I coordinate with my husband to take 1-2 nights away from the house every 3-4 months. When I'm away, I sleep, read, pray, take hikes or run, enjoy simple delicious food, and spend time with my thoughts. I recharge. Then, before the mom-cation is over, I schedule the next one. This is an important step. I look at the calendar my husband and I share and block off time.

There is no one-size fits all solution for everyone. Getting to know yourself and what is recharging for you will help you find your solutions. A recharge retreat can be for a few hours or a few days. It can happen weekly, monthly, quarterly, or yearly depending on your needs and the support you have.

- Do you recharge with friends? Plan time to connect with important relationships.

- Do you recharge by being alone? Plan quiet time for yourself.

- Does being in nature bring you energy and joy? Schedule time to get outside.

- Is curling up with a good book a way you recharge? Resist the urge to over work, or scroll on your phone once the kids are in bed and pull out a good book.

Your Turn:

Are you able to give yourself the non-sleep rest that you need? If you find that you struggle to get rejuvenating rest, then let's get serious about it together.

1. How often do you give yourself times of rest that aren't sleeping?

2. When did you last feel like you truly rested, and what were you doing?

3. What helps you to recharge?

Sleep

Don't skip over this section, thinking "sleep, ya right!" or "I'll sleep when I'm dead!" because I'm going to give you some tips and tools. Stories of sleep-deprived parents are not in short supply. If you are in a Parenting Marathon, the chances are good that your sleep is suffering. Are you losing sleep from kids that need attention multiple times a night, from worry or anxiety, or a burden of stress? How is your sleep health? If it's poor, there are steps you can take that will help your performance in this Parenting Marathon.

My friend Jamie has a compelling story about sleep and the crucial role it plays in our lives. Jamie's battle with sleep-deprivation crept in as a little evening cough one September day after the start of the new school year. By February, it had progressed to a nightmare. Jamie had just started back at her elementary school job after summer vacation. Her two young girls were in school or daycare while Jamie and her husband both worked. This little irritating evening cough worsened over the months. Work stress and hours of coughing in the evening kept Jamie awake until past midnight. An intense three-year-old woke her up multiple times each night before getting up for the day by 5:00 a.m. The night time hours contained cycles of sleep followed by restless periods of prolonged coughing. Her doctor didn't seem concerned, but by February, the lack of sleep came with profound feelings of hopelessness. She noticed that as a parent, her patience, creativity, and sense of humor were diminishing. Jamie confided in me that she felt like she was "losing it." Her mental health and physical health were in danger. "I feel like I'm wearing myself out from the inside," she told me.

Our bodies need sleep. Regardless of the specifics in your Parenting Marathon, *you* need sleep. Jamie, desperate to get answers and solutions, continued to advocate for herself. She changed doctors and persisted in being taken seriously for her worsening cough. Six months after the cough started, she was diagnosed with cough variant asthma. A treatment plan was initiated and she experienced her first full night of sleep in half a year! The difference that decent sleep had on restoring Jamie's physical and mental health was remarkable.

According to Chris Winter in *The Sleep Solution*, "Poor sleep is linked to a collection of problems, including obesity, increased risk of heart attack, high blood pressure, heart failure, stroke, depression, negative mood consequences, a variety of cancers and autoimmune disorders." Sleep is crucial to your health and you can take an active part in improving it.

If lack of sleep is part of your story right now, it's time to dig down deep and get creative with solutions. Your goal: 7-9 hours of peaceful sleep each night. Here are some things to consider to improve the quality of your sleep:

- Talk to your doctor about your sleep and be honest with him/her about your concerns. If your sleeplessness has a medical root, persevere to get answers and help.

- Find someone who can give you a night's break at least once a week so that you can sleep through the night without interruptions. Consider asking your partner, parent, close friend, or even hire help, then find a quiet spot in your home to sleep where you won't be disturbed.

- If your partner's habits consistently disrupt your sleep, consider what Dr. Chris Winter, author of *The Sleep Solution*, calls a "sleepcation": scheduled nights each week where you and your partner sleep apart in order to offer undisturbed sleep.

- Turn off screens at least two hours before you want to be asleep. Read paper books rather than books on tablets before bed time.

- Put some time and attention into making your room a peaceful sleeping den, including comfortable linens, cave darkness, and an absence of cell phones, tablets, TVs, and ticking clocks.

- Avoid caffeine six hours before your bedtime, and finish eating two hours before bed.

- Keep pets and kids out of your room during the night.

- Work towards a more consistent schedule for waking up and going to bed.

- If you have teens who seem to be ready for a second dinner at 10:00 p.m. and bedtime at midnight, consider going to bed before they do, and turn off Wi-Fi to eliminate the distraction for your teens.

Be ruthless in discovering what it takes to get enough restful sleep. You can't perform in a Parenting Marathon for long in a sleep deprived state.

Your Turn:

1. If sleep is an issue, write down two things you will do differently this week to get better sleep.

Step Two Quick Glance:

- Self-care is crucial during a Parenting Marathon.

- 3 Pauses is a daily recharging technique where you take 5-15 minutes, three times a day to do something that brings you energy, peace, or joy.

- Recharge Retreats are periodic, extended breaks from the stress of parenting. These can be a few hours or a few days, and can occur weekly, monthly, quarterly, or yearly. But they won't happen if you don't schedule them.

- Get serious about sleep. If you aren't sleeping well, review the suggestions, and make a plan to get the sleep you need in order to perform well in your Parenting Marathon.

"You are the author of your plan, so you get to edit it."

- DANA PARISI

Step Three:

MAKE A PLAN... BUT BE FLEXIBLE

You've probably heard the saying that "failing to plan is planning to fail." If we have goals we want to accomplish in our lives, including in our Parenting Marathon, making a plan is one of the first steps we should take. In training to run my first marathon, my plan was a detailed schedule typed out with specific miles to run each day, interval training workouts, strength training, and important REST days! I kept this plan taped to my wall in our dining room, where I saw it often. I took satisfaction in crossing off each workout as I accomplished them (yes, I'm one of those people who love to cross things off of lists). I didn't create this plan by myself, by the way. I had more experienced runners share their plans with me, and used their wisdom. So, I had a plan... excellent! But I couldn't always follow it to the letter. Some days the plan called for speed training, but the snow and ice on the path made anything more than a slow jog impossible. I got sick with a sinus infection that ended up with my lungs feeling clogged and heavy, and I struggled to breath just climbing a flight of stairs. Not ideal days for hill training, which was on my written plan. It was clear that I needed to learn to be flexible with my plan. I learned my lesson: make a plan and give yourself permission to make adjustments to that plan based on the current situation, **without** feeling guilty or defeated.

You are the author of your plan, so you get to edit it.

As my marathon training was reaching its longest miles, I suffered a foot injury that made walking painful, and I had to take two weeks off of running to recover. I had to edit my plan again. I swam (not my favorite activity), used a stationary bike, and did everything I could think of to aid my healing. Once I was recovered and back to running, the world entered the COVID-19 pandemic, and the local marathon I was training for was canceled. Back to editing the plan. But my practice with being flexible and rolling with the circumstances was helpful. Since I had trained, healed, and recovered my foot, I felt ready. The official race was canceled, so I edited my plan and ran the 26.2 miles in my own private marathon! Sure, it looked different than I had planned for, but crossing the "finish line" and being joined by my family who gave me a special medal made out of a can lid decorated with plastic beads was memorable!

As you navigate your Parenting Marathon, you are probably used to having plans change. Perhaps your child is falling apart in the store and you aren't able to finish your shopping. You may end up leaving a full cart in the aisle of the grocery store as you bring your child outside to help her calm down. Or you have a busy evening scheduled with getting three kids to their activities. As you rush to get the kitchen cleaned up after dinner, your son discovers he can't find the team shirt he needs and spirals into a meltdown, refusing to leave the house. Being flexible and able to calmly roll with life's changes, even as plans fall apart and need to be adjusted, is a skill that we can practice, improve, and model to our children. You don't need to be perfect at it; just be willing to be on the journey.

So what kind of planning does your particular Parenting Marathon need? Here are some possible plans you may consider for your situation.

- **Safety plan**: Make a safety plan if there are rages or behaviors that pose a threat to people or pets in the home.

- **Sleep plan**: See step 2 for reminders.

- **Sibling plan**: Does one child in your home take up 90% of the parental energy and time? You might need a plan to support the other kids in your home.

- **Relationship plan**: You are going to want to maintain your own close relationships during this Parenting Marathon for support and love. Make a plan to nurture your adult connections (more on that later).

- **Calm plan**: This plan means adding to your parenting toolbox of ways to help you stay calm, as well as ways to support your child's sense of well-being.

- **Meltdown plan**: If meltdowns are frequent, you can plan on another one happening. You'll feel better prepared, calm, and capable, if you have a plan on how to respond.

- **Transition plan(s)**: Many children struggle with transitions from one activity or situation to another. Transitioning to school, home from school, ending an activity to come to the dinner table, bath time, bed time, home from a friend's house or a sport, the end of screen time, and on and on. Transitions are everywhere. If transitions are hard for your child, make a plan and edit it as needed.

- **Summer plan**: Summer is usually thought of as a time of carefree days and fun. But for parents in a Parenting Marathon, it can be a lot of work and stress. You may need a summer plan.

- **Exit plan**: An exit plan is the plan you make and have in your back pocket if you need to leave the situation, event, or outing with your child who is struggling. An exit plan might be used if you're at a family holiday and one child is overwhelmed by the noise and stimulation. You may need an exit plan if you attempt to take your three kids to the park and one child is having a meltdown. These plans are specific for situations you think your child *might* struggle in.

- **Pregnancy plan**: If your family is expecting a new addition, then you have a lot to be excited about! You may also want to make some plans to help with this big transition.

- **Empty Nest plan**: Are you preparing for when your child leaves the home for work or school? This is a huge transition for parents. Take some time to consider what you want your weeks to include. Is there a new project or hobby you've been wanting to try? Are there interests and passions that have been set aside that you want to revisit? If you have a significant other, how do you want to nurture that relationship?

Don't panic about these different plans. You won't need all of them in any given Parenting Marathon. How many plans you consider at one time will vary. For example, if you have a spouse or co-parent then making a relationship plan will help you keep that foundation strong. That could look like a regular date night, time to catch up in the evening after work, or ways to communicate about plans, hopes, and expectations. At the same time, you might have a child that often has a meltdown after school, so you make a transition plan to ease the stress. Then, if you plan to go to a large family reunion that you think is likely to be overstimulating for your child, you make an exit plan for that situation.

You don't have to come up with these plans alone. Talk with the other trusted adults in your life and seek extra support through parenting books, a parent coach, or podcasts. I love helping parents make their plans, so please reach out if you'd like to brainstorm together.

Your Turn:

1. What sort of planning do you need to do for your Parenting Marathon?

2. Who can you ask to help you create your plans?

Step Three Quick Glance:

- Your Parenting Marathon will require some planning.

- When it comes to making your plans, don't forget you can get help from people you trust.

- Be willing to be flexible and edit your plans as needed.

"*There is no one right way to measure your progress. Any way you decide to do it will work. The important point is that you do some type of measurement.*"

— JERRY BRUCKNER

Step Four:

KEEP TRACK AND WATCH FOR
PROGRESS AND PATTERNS

As I've mentioned, I haven't been a life-long runner. In fact, for years, I hated the idea of running. Why would someone torture themselves like that? The idea of joining the women's running group came to me in church one day. Our church was hosting a "small group rally" to encourage everyone to find their community within our large church. As I looked through all of the wonderful group options available the thought occurred to me that what I really craved was a group of women to be active with. The group that came to my mind was the running group, so I joined. As it turned out, I wasn't terrible as a new runner, but it was hard work! I envied the women who made it look so effortless, the ones who could hold a full conversation as we ran and ran. I coped by asking them questions, so they could do the talking, and I could focus on breathing!

Early on, I started keeping track of my running miles and pace. At first it was out of curiosity: How many miles would I run in the week, the month? But what quickly became evident was that I was finding encouragement by the progress I was unknowingly recording. My running journal kept track of the facts: miles, pace, even the "feels like" temperature, and the layers I wore for running as the weather got colder. I also recorded a little note about more subjective things like how I felt during the run. Did the run go by in the blink of an eye and I felt great? Maybe a run dragged on and I felt like my legs were made out of lead. I kept track of my running fuel. It seemed ridiculous to me at first that I would need to bring food along on our runs. But as I talked to more seasoned runners and got their suggestions, I started trying out different options for myself, and taking notes. I learned that I felt the best if I had around 100 calories every four miles of running. A lot of what I learned was through trial and error. I would wear too many layers on a winter run and be uncomfortably warm. The next run, I would be dressed too lightly and stay cold the whole time. I deal with cold and exercise induced asthma, and I learned at exactly what temperature I needed to use my inhaler before I ran. I even recorded how I recovered after a long run. I learned a lot about myself, what worked well for me, and just as importantly, what didn't work well for me. I was on a self-discovery journey, and these are the exact tools I needed for my Parenting Marathons.

My first Parenting Marathon record keeping didn't start out of mere curiosity, like my running record keeping. It bloomed out of fear. Our struggles with our daughter were getting more concerning. We were seeing an increased pattern of unhealthy survival behaviors like lying, stealing, destroying things, screaming, and aggression. Our daughter would often accuse my husband or I of "always yelling," being mean and unfair. At the time, I didn't fully understand how early life experiences had contributed to my child's brain being wired for hyper-vigilance. Heightened alertness for signs of threat can lead a child to misinterpret an adult's serious tone as yelling or being threatening. We were experiencing daily struggles. One meltdown led to another, and by the end of a week, I couldn't remember what started any of them.

I decided to keep a small notebook to describe the issues I was seeing. I started keeping this record as a way of recording the facts, looking for patterns, and watching to see if the behaviors were consistent or getting worse. I wanted a record of my clearest memory of each day because the days and struggles blended into each other. I would look back at the day exhausted and wonder how things went from calm to chaos so fast. What triggered that meltdown in the first place?

Parent Detective:

I started seeing myself as a detective. I was taking field notes in the wild jungle of my family life! I wrote down things about the meltdowns: what happened leading up to each one, how long it lasted, what happened during the meltdown, and how I tried to manage it. I also paid attention to the sibling dynamics during times of struggle. If you have more than one child, then you can relate to the domino effect on siblings. It starts with one child who is having a tough time. That child does something that stresses out another child, who then reacts in a way that increases the stress in the first. The more kids you have, the more dominos to collide with each other.

My detective "field notes" included what I tried to do to help my kids calm down. It was especially helpful to note which things I tried helped defuse the situation, as well as which things tended to make the situation worse. There was no pre-written manual for what I was going through, just like there's not an exact manual for what you're going through.

It took time for me to make this parenting record. And my days were already full and exhausting. I spent a little time each evening jotting down notes about what happened during that day. Waiting to make my notes until the next day, or 3 days later, didn't help me. We were experiencing so many meltdowns and struggles each day that they would blend into each other and the facts would get blurred. Taking the time each night meant I had the most accurate recollection of the situation. Although it took time, it gave me a bigger picture of what we were dealing with. Patterns started to emerge. I started making small adjustments in my days based on what had worked and what hadn't worked in previous similar situations.

As a parent, I was also doing a lot of studying and learning during this season. My empathy for children who have experienced trauma *and* their parents soared. My husband and I had navigated a few Parenting Marathons with our children prior to this season. I thought back to some of them and realized that when we hit roadblocks in other Parenting Marathons, I tended to seek out more resources. For example, when our oldest child was in third grade, we finally started connecting the dots to his excessive energy, lack of focus, and disorganization. I read everything I could find about ADHD (Attention-deficit/hyperactivity disorder), talked with his doctor, and set off on a plan to get him some needed help. I was now on a different "race course" than others I had experienced before, but it was just another version of a Parenting Marathon. Although each Parenting Marathon we go through is unique, there are many commonalities.

In regards to understanding our daughter's behaviors and struggles, I still hadn't found resources that led to the solutions I needed. A lot of the common parenting wisdom out there, including things that worked fairly well for our older two kids, was backfiring in this new Parenting Marathon. Our children who were adopted had different early life experiences than our biological kids. Neither is right or wrong, but I needed a better understanding. I needed to understand the root issues to the challenging behaviors so I could be more effective in coaching my kids. I was determined to persevere. One crucial step I took was hiring a parent coach. I'll admit now that it was one of the most humbling things I've done on my parenting journey.

I felt like I was an experienced enough parent, so it bothered me that I was struggling. *"I should be able to figure this out."* It felt like a failure to admit that many of my attempts to connect with my daughter and redirect explosive behavior seemed to be making things worse. Accepting help was very hard for me. Looking back at that season now from a healthier, more joyful spot in my parenting journey, I would love to go back and tell my earlier self that there is no shame in seeking expert advice. In fact, it was a brilliant plan to find someone who had gone before me on a similar Parenting Marathon, and get their advice and lessons learned. You would probably never consider "re-inventing the wheel" for your car, when there are lots and lots of wheels out there that you can implement. When it comes to your Parenting Marathon, learning from someone who has gone before you, done the research, and experienced success, will shorten your trajectory to success yourself.

Working with a parent coach and diving into understanding early life trauma and how it can affect the brain and behavior, I started implementing more calm and connected parenting strategies. And, I started seeing positive changes. I was encouraged by looking through my "Parent Detective Notebook" and picking out concrete signs of growth! The meltdowns became less explosive and shorter over time. I was able to stay calmer and more present in the tough moments and all of my kids started to calm down with help easier. Things that used to set off a meltdown no longer caused the same reaction. After rough interactions, I was also able to "reset" myself more quickly. Whereas in the past I would have held a grudge and felt exhausted and resentful for the outburst we had just navigated, now I was finding myself feeling steadier. I was calming down more quickly, focusing on the positives, and being able to re-engage my kids into positive interactions. We were more connected and working together. All this time, I had been unknowingly recording progress!

Seeing how this record keeping was helping me with this particular Parenting Marathon, I started recording the facts about challenges with my other kids as well. (Names are changed.)

For example:

"Jon was unable to focus this morning to get ready for school on time." And I started to see patterns emerge. *"He got distracted when he went downstairs to brush his teeth and forgot the rest of the steps he needed to do to be ready for school."* You can probably guess that some patterns became identifiable. Children with ADHD are often more distractible and have difficulty with executive functioning skills like organizing, sequencing, and planning. My son often ran into trouble focusing on his tasks in the morning. Recognizing this helped me make simple changes that affected every school day. We started keeping his toothbrush on the main floor, so he didn't have to go down to the lower level where his room and bathroom were located and possibly (or likely) get distracted. Now, that perhaps is merely a quick "bandage" fix over the bigger issue of his concentration and distractibility, but the small change made our mornings smoother.

"Mary was irritable every morning this week, said hurtful things to siblings, was quick to complain or argue, and was easily upset by the normal noise of siblings. This lasted until after she had breakfast, then she seemed calmer." Using that data, we made a few adjustments to her morning routine that may

seem silly to you, but that helped get us through those rough patches. I started waking her up by handing her a protein bar and giving her the option to have a little food in her room before joining the bustle of the main rooms, thus avoiding her coming out hangry (angry from being hungry). Then we let her choose to sit alone in a quieter room for breakfast if she wanted to ease into the day without the noise of the rest of the family. We used these personalized solutions for as long as we needed them, and then they just naturally phased out. The changes had served their purpose and the mornings continued to go more smoothly.

Record keeping helped me recognize growth in problem solving with my daughter to get through meltdowns.

"Rachel screamed and started pushing me when I reminded her to clean up her room after school. Episode lasted 3 hours. Ended when I sat in the room with her, and walked her through the steps to pick up her room one by one, doing the steps together. "Let's pick up all the dirty clothes and put them in the hamper together. Great! Now let's toss the toys in their box. Now all we have left are the scraps of paper, let's put them in the trash." Actual work of cleaning her room with my guidance was 10 minutes."

My detective notes also helped me reflect back on things that I did that tended to make a meltdown worse for one of my kids and which things helped calm that child down.

"Got into a "last word battle" accidently with Jack today. He was angry about me saying no to ice cream before dinner and said: "You're the worst mom.""

Already frustrated, I said "I guess I'm just the worst."

He screamed, "stop it!"

I responded, "I'm stopping."

He screamed "STOP!"

I said "yup"

(I'm embarrassed to say it went on longer than that!)

Looking back, I was sort of poking the bear. I should have just dropped the silly "last word battle."

I recorded honestly how the struggles were affecting me: when I felt resentful, exhausted, fearful, sad, or confused. But the most joy came when I started recognizing and recording the progress!

"Rachel looked like she was going to have a meltdown when it was time for reading homework. I offered her some warm tea and suggested we tag team and read every other page. We read for 10 minutes before she started to lose focus, get whiny and fidgety. We ended our reading earlier than I planned but with no meltdown!"

Your Turn:

1. Pick a notebook (paper or digital) and start your Parent Detective notebook. Record the last meltdown, argument or challenge in your home. What set things off? What happened during the interaction? How long did it last? How did your child start to recover and how long did the recovery take? Record any info you think would be helpful. This doesn't have to be award-winning writing. Make short notes and keep it simple.

Step Four Quick Glance:

- Keep track of the struggles to uncover patterns and to see progress.

- If your child is struggling with challenging behaviors or frequent meltdowns, put on your parent detective hat, get curious, and pay attention to the triggers.

"Simplicity is making the journey of this life with just baggage enough."

- CHARLES WARNER

Step Five:

SIMPLIFY

Simplify Schedules

Do you ever wonder how your life got so complicated? Parenting Marathon seasons are good times to look at ways to simplify.

Marathon training, as you can guess, requires a commitment of time. In order to train for my first marathon, I aimed to do four runs a week including one "long run" which slowly increased in mileage over the three-month training period. This was sort of the perfect year for me to train for a marathon because it was the year I mentioned earlier, when my youngest child was in half day 4K, four mornings a week. After having young kids at home with me consistently for 13 years, I finally had a "window" of time that was open. I found that my success in making these runs happen depended on me writing my runs into our calendar, just like I do for my kids' activities. It helped me keep that space on my calendar available for training rather than filling it up with other chores or requests for my time. Think about that for a second. Maybe even open up your calendar and take a look at your week. Do you have various things scheduled for your children? Looking at my calendar right now, I have scheduled tutoring, athletic events, church youth group, and doctor's appointments in the next week for my kids. Sadly, there is something scheduled every day. And the reality is that the things we schedule in our calendar are typically the things we prioritize and make sure happen. If, for example, you schedule teacher conferences for your child, either you have an excellent memory and retain the date and time in your head, or you record the information on some form of calendar. You schedule it to guard that time.

Before I started training for this marathon, I hardly ever included something for myself in the weekly calendar. It seemed selfish to record a block of time for a workout for myself. But why is that? My children's sports and activities were a priority to me. I made adjustments all the time to make sure they got to their activities, not to mention birthday parties and playdates. I had to make the mindset shift that my activities, priorities, and health were also worth scheduling time for. The running group that I had joined gave me the perfect "excuse" I needed to start carving out time for myself. Not that I needed an excuse technically, but in my head I felt like I did. Since my running group was an activity that I paid for, it gave me extra motivation to ensure I was making the most out of my purchase. I tend to be frugal at heart and hate wasting money by buying something I don't use. On my calendar, each person's activities are marked by a different color. So, I chose a color for myself and started to schedule in my running times. My consistency with guarding that time to run with my group, or even by myself, significantly increased the more I practiced. My family could clearly see, on the dry erase board version of a calendar that we keep in the dining room, when my runs were scheduled. It felt to me that my husband was more accepting of me taking the time to step out of the house for a run when it was clearly scheduled on the calendar than when I planned it last minute and announced I was taking a short run. Scheduling in time for my runs was important, but as we all know, there are only so many hours in a week.

I needed to simplify in other areas of my life for a season. Take a look at your own calendar. What's on it? When it comes to my "calendar clutter," I tend to go in waves. There will be a season when I feel like the sky's the limit. "Yes! I can take that on!," "Count me in!," "Yes, I can squeeze that in too!" From driving kids to their activities, making treats for a gathering, volunteering at schools and church, to serving on the board of something, my free time can get sucked up. Eventually, a switch flips inside me and I look at my calendar and panic. "I'm doing too much! I'm always exhausted and running around all over town like a mad person! I need to ditch EVERYTHING extra on my calendar!" Then, in my stress, I start unloading obligations, saying no to invitations and seeking a quieter calendar. However, because I rarely seem to find "the sweet spot", where I have just the right amount of activities and obligations, I find I'm right back to the beginning, filling every blank space on the calendar and overextending myself once again.

Parenting Flat Tires

Most Parenting Marathons aren't things we take on with advanced planning like marathon training for running. Although some Parenting Marathons may be predicted, many of mine seem to sneak up on me. They might start with a collection of smaller challenges that I call "parenting flat tires."

Over the course of two winters, my husband and I bought used downhill ski equipment for the family and started teaching the kids how to ski. One Saturday, while my husband worked, I decided to meet my dad at the ski hill and enjoy a beautiful Midwest winter day with my three oldest kids while my youngest had a special Grandma day. The ski day was a success and we spent more time on the hill than we normally would because everyone was having fun. Finally, it was time to pack up our ski gear and carry it to the van so we could get back to my parents' house for dinner, pick up my youngest, say our goodbyes, and make the two-hour trip back to our house (preferably in plenty of time for showers and normal bed time). The plan made perfect sense in my head, and I didn't see any reason for it to be a problem. But I had missed the signs of an advancing storm brewing in my daughter.

My dad left the ski hill in his car with my son while the two girls and I worked on getting our equipment together to leave. I noticed that my younger daughter was struggling to stay calm. She was tired from the active day outside and frustrated trying to organize her ski gear. As she waited for me to help her, she started feeling cold and thirsty. Once everyone's gear was collected from the ski racks, it was awkward and challenging for her to carry her skis and poles. My hands were overflowing with my boots, skis and poles, her boots, and our oversized family gear bag, so I didn't have a free hand to help her carry her skis. Her whining turned more urgent and angry as we tried to inch towards the parking lot. We were in view of my van, so I told her to put her gear down by the fence and we would come back to get it when my hands were free. Maybe she didn't hear me, or maybe she wasn't able to change course, but she kept trudging along, hauling her ski equipment.

By the time we lurched our way to the van and stowed away the gear, she was in "shutdown" mode. She refused to get into the van. Instead, she stood with a scowl on her face outside the van door. I tried coaxing and comforting but she could not be reasoned with. I tried tempting her with a warm ride and a snack, but that failed. I tried insisting she get in the van... nope. It was getting colder, and my other daughter and I were getting chilled (and frustrated) waiting for her to climb in. I knew I couldn't pick her up and put her in the van because she would just open the door and jump back out. So, I reassured her that I wasn't going to leave her, but I *was* going to close the sliding van door to stay warmer until she was ready to come in. As the van door started to slide shut, she blocked it so that it popped back open. She wouldn't let the door close and she wouldn't come in. She also wouldn't look at me or talk to me other than to yell that I was mean. My daughter sitting inside the van was also tired and cold from the day. Hungry and anxious to get to dinner, she became frustrated with her sister and started falling apart too, complaining loudly that I was "allowing" this crazy behavior. My plan for the evening was derailing. As I sat in my unmoving, cold van, with the sliding door open, my two girls angry and upset, one inside the van and the other refusing to get in, the thought crossed my mind that I was experiencing a "parenting flat tire."

If you've ever experienced a flat tire on your car while driving, you know how much it stinks. You also know **it is going to slow you down**. You may feel mad at the tire for popping, you may have a tight time frame and are going to be late for something important, but nothing is going to change the fact that you must slow down. Whether you're a pro at changing your car's tire, or you need to call for help, a flat tire is an inconvenience. It's going to take extra time, maybe a lot of extra time. I've only had one flat tire on my car. I ran over something sharp on the road and heard a loud flapping sound. Instantly I could tell what had happened. Thankfully, I was only a mile from my home and I was able to pull over safely. I'm a bit embarrassed to say I'm not confident in my tire changing skills, so I called my husband who thankfully was home. It was only a few minutes before he joined us and started changing the tire to the spare for me. As flat tire experiences go, I was lucky, but it was still inconvenient. It made me late and frustrated.

This "parenting flat tire" that popped up at the end of our ski day was going to take some time, just like fixing a real flat tire. I didn't know how long it would take, but I didn't have any other option than to wait. I didn't want to make things worse, and somehow I needed to start fixing this "flat." I offered my older daughter a snack and a drink while she waited in the van. I opened up our emergency car blanket to wrap her in so she was more comfortable. I took some slow deep breaths to center myself, then I stepped outside to be with my younger daughter. Since I was outside with her, she didn't stop me from closing the door, so I could keep the inside of the van a little warmer. I moved slowly and kept my words few and calm as I tested the waters to see if my daughter would allow me to comfort her. She let me give her a side hug, and I softly said, "I love you sweetie." I didn't say anything else. I resisted the urge to lecture or order her around. I reminded myself that a flat tire takes time, and being upset about it doesn't change that fact. I adjusted my mindset from feeling mad and inconvenienced to finding empathy for my daughter who was struggling. I waited. Eventually, wordlessly, she climbed in the van, buckled up, and accepted a snack. Our "flat tire" was fixed. We were back on the road, but quite a bit more worn out from the experience.

The day after the ski day "parenting flat tire," I was able to look at the factors leading up to my daughter going into "shutdown" mode and see some of the triggers. Hindsight is a gift we don't have in the present moment, but if I had the day to do over again, I would have made some simple changes. Although we had a great time skiing, I would have wisely ended a little earlier, while my kids still had some energy and reserves. Knowing how frustrating it is to juggle ski gear, I might have asked my dad to wait with the kids while I made multiple trips and loaded all of our gear, freeing them up to walk unburdened through the icy parking lot. Even though we can't go back and use the insight we gained during our "parenting flat tire" moments, we can incorporate that insight into future flat tires.

Parenting Marathons often encompass multiple "parenting flat tire" moments in a given season. A Parenting Marathon can sap your energy reserves. If you are in a Parenting Marathon, it's time to take a look at all of your commitments and redefine your priorities. There will be other, less challenging seasons where you can say yes to those extras but this is the time to focus your efforts on the most crucial things. It's triage time. We live in a culture that wears "busy" as a badge of honor. It takes conscious effort to fight against the pull to be constantly busy and productive or to have your kids participating in all the options available for kids these days. It can also take courage to say "no" when people make additional requests of your time and energy. If people in your life are used to you saying "yes" to their requests, it may be hard for them when you become more selective. You might experience some "push back." But in a marathon season, you need to build extra cushion time into your day as preparation for possible struggles, "parenting flat tires," and meltdowns. Some of my most frustrating parenting moments have come when I have a tightly packed evening planned: kids home from school at 4:00 p.m.; dinner promptly at 5:00 p.m. so the kids can eat, clean up, and get prepared for swim team at 6:00 p.m., which means we need to leave no later than 5:45 p.m. to make it on time. On an evening like this, I don't have time for one child to melt down at 5:43 p.m. because their favorite swimsuit is still in a wet stinky heap at the bottom of their swim bag. Since I'm rushing around to clean up the dinner mess before we leave, I'm also not as patient and empathetic as I would like to be. My response of "just grab another suit and let's go! We're going to be late" does not help in slowing the parenting flat tire that threatens to rupture the evening plans.

So, what needs to change? I used to think it made me feel fulfilled to cross everything off my to-do list. I even added things to the list that I had already done, just so I could cross them off! But that laser focus on accomplishing tasks put me on the hamster wheel of running for a false destination. To-do lists really can just go on and on. There is more work for tomorrow and always more things that *could* be done today. What can *you* do to simplify your calendar and schedule, and slow down your pace and the pace of your family during a Parenting Marathon season? Each one of us will have a different answer to this question, but to get you started, here are some things that I did to simplify.

- I made peace with blank squares on my calendar. Typically, when I see a blank day on my calendar, I see it as an opportunity to plan something! In a Parenting Marathon, I see it as a blessing, a quiet day of rest.

- I talked with each kid about the activities they were in and narrowed things down to one activity per child at a time.

- I became more proactive with coordinating carpools with other parents to cut down on my running around. When that wasn't possible, I had times when I paid a college student to do pick-ups or drop-offs for the older kids' activities, so I could stay home with the younger kids, rather than dragging them to every event, and trying to keep them quiet and busy from the sidelines as we watched the older kids.

- Other times, I organized some babysitter evenings, so the younger kids could have fun at home rather than join me watching an older kid's event.

- During that particularly challenging year when I homeschooled my younger daughter, I had the least "free time" for myself. I finally built into our homeschool day a break for myself and prioritized quiet, recharging time. When my husband was home from work, I took opportunities to get out of the house and do something that helped my mental health like exercise or a visit with a friend.

- I was ruthless in saying "no" to all extra requests, including good things I typically was happy to do like volunteering at church or the kids' schools, making treats for an event or helping out with a fundraiser. (If you find this challenging, remind yourself that this is only for a season, you can return to doing some of those "extras" later.)

What I discovered was that joy comes when I can slow down for the little moments in the day. Things like laughing at the silly statement my daughter made, or seeing the light in my son's eyes when he knows that I'm really listening to his story rather than the old "half-listen" while I multi-task doing the dishes and paying bills. I was finding it easier to stay patient and connected to each of my kids. If there is something going on in your life that requires significant time and energy, then this is the time to take a fresh look at your commitments and simplify in the areas you can. Whether that "something" is there by your choice (like running marathon training) or by circumstances you can't control (Parenting Marathons), it's demanding room in your life. It's time to triage.

Your Turn:

1. What needs to change in your schedule so you can be more present and focus on helping your child through a difficult season?

2. What help can you access to decrease your work and stress load?

3. What things on your calendar are causing you or your kids the most stress?

4. Which adjustment do you want to start making THIS week?

Simplify Spaces:

We've talked about simplifying schedules. Now let's look at simplifying spaces. When I was training for my marathon, it didn't take long for me to realize that where I run makes a difference in how I feel about the run. A run in a location I don't know well, with lots of traffic lights and road crossings, makes for a more stressful run for me than a well-known bike path, or a peaceful trail in a county park. When I run on the bike path I'm familiar with, I don't have to think about where to go, or watch for traffic. I can run and let my mind relax. The space is "simpler" and therefore more peaceful for me. Let's translate that into the spaces we live in and find what makes for a peaceful space for you.

We all have different comfort levels with clutter and mess in our homes. My mom is a "stacker." If all of her papers, mail, cook books, and miscellaneous items are stacked in neat piles, she is happy. I am a "sweeper." When there are unnecessary items left on any horizontal surface in my house, I want to sweep them all in a bag and get them out of sight. Counter tops, tables, the top of my washer and dryer, the shoe bench in the front hallway... all are landing places for random items that belong someplace else. Homework, mittens, snack plates, wrappers, paper scraps, markers, glue sticks, mail, keys, chargers, and books are all likely to end up on my kitchen table over the course of a single day. There isn't one right way to organize your space, but take some time to think about what makes for a stress-free space in your home for you. Consider the room you tend to gravitate towards when you need to recharge or find peace. For me, an uncluttered room helps me relax. Sitting down in my kitchen when all the surfaces are littered with objects, I find it impossible to relax. Perhaps you or someone you know seems to be a totally different, more relaxed, fun-loving person when they're away from their home and on vacation. Of course vacations are meant to be fun, but a big factor in the change of personality has to do with decreased stress and obligations, as well as simplified spaces and expectations.

My family took a trip to sunny San Diego one Christmas break. We decided to escape Wisconsin winter for a week and explore a new area. On this trip, we stayed in a vacation rental home. It was actually more of an apartment. The space was small and had no view, but it was clean and simple, and it felt so peaceful. Truly, the apartment was nothing special. Its peacefulness came from the simplicity of the space. It wasn't cluttered. There were no piles of things to manage or extra things collecting on counters that didn't seem to have a proper place. I asked my husband, "What would it take to make our home feel more peaceful like a vacation rental?" We decided to work on our living room with the goal of a clean, simple, clutter-free space. Although it takes effort to battle the clutter that wants to settle in our "vacation rental-like living room," the efforts are worthwhile. In daily moments when I have time to pause, I find joy and peace in the simplified space.

Consider helping your child simplify their own space as well. Does their bedroom have too many things in it for them to be able to take care of? Work together to discover what would make their space feel peaceful for them. You probably know how it feels when you have a task that needs to get done that feels enormous. Our kids' rooms can become that task for them when their things get out of hand. Have you ever sent your child off to their room telling them to clean it up, and then came back later to find the room exactly the same? Perhaps you also see your child contently playing on the floor? Maybe they simply got distracted, or perhaps the task felt so daunting they didn't know how to get started, and so they stayed stuck. You are the expert on your child. Would it work best to straighten up and simplify their room together? Maybe while they're away, you can step in and do a few things to simplify the space, and return it to a peaceful baseline that will be easier for your child to maintain.

Your Turn:

1. What does a peaceful, relaxing space look like for you?

2. What space in your home do you go to when you want to relax? (If you don't have a space yet, which space would you want to consider?)

3. What could you do in that space to make it more peaceful?

4. What can you and your child do to simplify his/her space and make it more peaceful?

Step Five Quick Glance:

- Parenting Marathons take time and energy. Look for ways you can simplify.
- Consider how you can simplify your and your family's schedules and obligations.
- It's ok to say "no" to some of the requests you get.
- "Parenting flat tires" are frustrating and take extra time. Build some extra cushion time into your days.
- Simplify a space in your home and see the impact it has.

"*If you want to go fast, go alone; if you want to go far, go together.*"

- **AFRICAN PROVERB**

Step Six:
GET SUPPORT

There is so much to learn when you pick up a new hobby or activity. Although the mechanics of running, and therefore marathon training, seem simple enough–just put one foot in front of the other... over and over again–there was still a lot for me to learn. I picked the brains of experienced long-distance runners about things like fueling and hydration, running shoes, recovery, speed work, and mental race strategies. I learned things about foot care, and preventing chafing (ok I concede, non-runners, you have reason to think we are crazy). Having people who would share their knowledge and experience with me meant I didn't have to "reinvent the wheel" and "discover" all the answers by trial and error. I could move forward faster on the learning curve. The support and advice I got from my running friends was invaluable. I also had support at home. It takes a commitment of time to train for a marathon. I had my new system of simplifying my commitments and scheduling in my running times, but I still needed the support of my family. Although I tried to sneak my runs in during the small window of time when all my kids were at school, it still impacted my family. I found myself extra tired and sometimes crabby after my long runs. My husband picked up some more parental tasks to make it possible for me to get in my training runs. I certainly needed support while I trained.

During a marathon race, support is also key. Support stations are set up along the way to provide water, fuel, or medical assistance. Six miles into my first in-person marathon, I approached a "fuel station" where volunteers were handing out little packs of gel or gummy food sources. A high-school-aged volunteer was ready for the hand off! As I reached for a package of what are basically fruit snacks for runners, we missed and the fruit snacks fell on the path. I kept running, figuring I'd have another chance later, but the volunteer was determined! He picked up the package and raced after me yelling "Don't worry, I've got it!" He caught up to me, placed the little pouch firmly in my hand, and I was on my way. It warmed my heart that he put in that extra effort to support me when it would have been easier for him to simply wait for the next runner to go by. In a Parenting Marathon, we need to have support stations along the way, as well.

I first started to recognize my need for support after a big family move for a new job. At the time, we had two kids, ages three and four. Three months after our move, I found myself crying in a therapist's office. I am not one who's quick to cry, and I actually had never talked to a therapist before that day. At a recent appointment with my new family doctor, she had asked me how things were going after our move, and to my dismay, my facade cracked and the struggles I was dealing with came tumbling out. My doctor encouraged me to talk with a therapist, and here I was. As I fought to gain control of the floodgates of my tears (feeling so embarrassed), the therapist shared interesting statistics about the timeframe for adjusting to a new town, and the process of grieving for the place that was left.

But that wasn't my particular struggle at the time. Our move was anticipated with joy. My husband was finally done with his education and starting his first professional job. We loved the city we moved to, our kids' new school, our neighbors, and our new church. We already felt like we were connecting and making new friends. Everything about the change would have been perfect except that our four-year-old son was experiencing intense anxiety following our move. Always a sensitive child, and an out-of-the-box sort of kid, I sought to help prepare him and our three-year-old daughter for the move. We read books about their favorite characters moving. We visited our new town, and did somersaults in the empty family room of our new home. We imagined which wall we would put their beds next to in their new bedrooms and pictured life in our new location. We took pictures of key people and places from the town we were leaving and I made a photo album of memories for each of the kids. Trying to anticipate the needs of a sensitive child, I thought I had hit the ball out of the park on this one. I felt that I had thought of everything and was prepared for a smooth transition.

I'm not sure how long it was after we settled into our new home that my son started struggling with anxiety and separation fears. It started with little things and grew. He became terrified if he couldn't see me, even when we were in the house together. He wouldn't play in a room that I wasn't in. The new "play area" of our house, that I was so excited about, went unused unless I was with him in that space as well. On one occasion, I got both kids bundled up in their car seats to head out for groceries and then I realized I had forgotten my phone in the house. It only took me 30 seconds to run in and grab the phone, but I returned to a little boy in a full panic attack. I had never seen a panic attack before, but there was no other way to describe it. He was sobbing, sweating, and terrified. When I drew the line at having him join me in the bathroom at home, he would lay on the floor outside the door watching for my reflection on the shiny bathroom tiles. "What are you doing?" I would ask when I heard him sliding around the floor outside the bathroom door. "Just making sure I know where you are," he'd reply. "Where do you think I could go? There's not even a window in this bathroom," I laughed. "Just waiting for you," came his response.

I tried reassurance. I occasionally got frustrated. His fear and hyper-vigilant behavior were exhausting me. On the rare occasions when he was able to play with his little sister just outside of visual range from me, he would "ping" like a submarine sonar.

"MOMMY?!"

"Yes?"

"Oh, nothing......MOMMY?!"

"What?"

"OK"

And on and on.

If I walked too fast through the house to get ready, or to clean up, he would panic as he tried to keep up with me. As a parent I felt stuck. I felt embarrassed that I was struggling and too proud to admit we had a real problem. "I should be able to handle this," I thought over and over. I was slow to seek help.

I never intended to bring it up at that routine checkup with my new family medicine doctor. In fact, I was caught off guard by her sincere inquiry into our transition after our move, causing me to let my guard down and finally share some of the emotions I was feeling. Later, sitting in the therapist's office, delving deeper into the struggles we were experiencing, I expected her to just listen and be empathetic. To my surprise, she got me started on the path to get help for my son. She set the wheels in motion to have him see a child therapist, who after meeting us once, recognized as a little atypical some of the behaviors we had come to experience as normal. During the one session that we met with the child therapist, our son was entertaining. He was articulate and talked about a wide variety of subjects with a larger than expected vocabulary for a 4-year-old. He moved his body non-stop in her office, including throwing his back against my husband's chest while sitting in front of him, repetitively like he was drumming. He inspected every object on her shelves and then seated himself under her wooden art easel while we talked. I thought he was just playing in a made-up fort, but he was actually unscrewing all the wing nuts of her art easel and inspecting how the art easel was made. The therapist got a kick out of him. When she saw the art easel taken apart, she politely encouraged him, for his next challenge, to try to put it back together. He did. Then she *encouraged us* to meet with a pediatric occupational therapist. One more stop on the "support train" for us. The occupational therapist was instrumental in recognizing our son's sensory processing disorder and helping us learn tools and techniques that benefited him in many areas of his life, including calming this recent separation anxiety he was experiencing. Support came from many sources, but it couldn't start until I was ready to admit we needed it.

As we journey on our Parenting Marathons, we need to be active in seeking out support for ourselves and our child. Find people who have knowledge and experience with what you are dealing with. Don't wait, hoping things will magically get better. Don't let embarrassment or fear hold you back from your opportunity for growth and progress. There are many avenues that could provide some of the support you need: medical professionals, counselors, physical and occupational therapists, vision therapists, dietitians, and individualized educational plans to address school struggles are just a few.

Support also includes friends and family in your life who are on your side during good times and hard times. The more honest I've been willing to be with my trusted friends and family about the struggles I am dealing with, the more supported I have felt. Don't do your Parenting Marathon in isolation from caring adults who you can trust. But at the same time, be choosy about who you share with, and let them know if you are sharing in confidentiality. Your child probably doesn't need the whole world to know all the details about their situation, so perhaps avoid shouting your struggle to the masses on social media. Remember, there are people who will make judgments about you and your child based on what you share, or offer up quick and easy solutions without fully understanding your unique situation, so share with discretion to people you know you can trust.

Support comes in lots of different forms. There's professional support and emotional support, but don't be afraid to ask for some practical daily support as well. That might mean accepting a meal, a ride for your child, or some child care. Even family members who live far away can give you support. I used to text my mom and ask her to make a grandma video call to one of my kids who needed some extra love. Get creative in the different ways you can get support.

Your Turn:

1. Make a list of the current support you have for this marathon. List professional support, as well as friends and family that provide emotional support.

2. Are there types of support you should consider for your child or for yourself as you journey on this Parenting Marathon?

3. Is there a support person that you should contact this week? Put a reminder in your calendar now.

Supporting parents on their journey is what I LOVE to do. If you could use additional support, please reach out. Remember that I have a special page of free resources for you at www.ParentingMarathon. com/resources. There you will find the downloadable workbook, bonus free training video, and more. You can also reach out to me on that site, or find me at www.LivesTouchedCoaching.com.

Step Six Quick Glance:

- Everyone in a Parenting Marathon needs support.

- Support comes in many different forms and from many different sources.

- Look for people who can provide professional, emotional, or practical support.

"Try to be a rainbow in someone else's cloud."

- MAYA ANGELOU

Step Seven:

FOCUS ON THE POSITIVES

"Aim to drink 80 ounces of water each day for the three days before the marathon."

"Get to bed early."

"Don't try any new foods that could bother your stomach the day before the race."

"Trim your toenails"

And, "NO NEGATIVITY!"

These were all useful bits of advice I got from experienced runners prior to my first half-marathon. Although many of the suggestions made sense as far as being prepared physically for my race, the "no negativity" advice stuck with me the most. Our minds are powerful tools.

We have all experienced times when we've felt grumpy or sad, and then seem to find more and more things that make us more and more grumpy and sad. Long-distance runners occasionally talk about a phenomenon that can occur during the taper period of training (days or weeks of decreased physical exertion

91

right before a big race). They can experience persistent, annoying pains that weren't present during the training period. These irritating pains, or "niggles," can become the catalyst to negative thinking and self-talk heading into the race. "No negativity! Only positive thoughts!" is the way to move forward on race day.

I have some running friends that love to talk about race strategy. I was lucky enough to get to grab a drink with them the week before that first half-marathon and listen to different strategies for pace, mindset, motivation, and perseverance. Part of my race day strategy was to write, in permanent marker on my arm, the names of 13 friends and family members who I was going to think about and pray for, one mile at a time. When I started feeling tired or discouraged at mile 8, I looked at my arm and saw my sister's name. Focusing on praying for her kept my mind from swirling towards negative thoughts like "I can't do this anymore," "I'm not good enough," and "what was I thinking?!"

There have been many winter training runs when I'm still far from home and feel like quitting (which obviously is problematic when it's 10 degrees out). I keep myself moving by thinking of all the things I have to be grateful for that day, or week, or month. Since I'm trying to keep myself moving back to the warmth of my home, I start with gratitude for the ability to run...and a warm place to call home. I also love to keep in mind three things that I'm looking forward to. When I run with friends, I love to ask them "what are three things you're looking forward to? The three things can be big or small, near or far." Even in the toughest Parenting Marathons, you can still find three small things to look forward to! Give it a try.

Your Turn:

1. What about you? We don't need to be running 13 miles together for me to ask. What are three things that you are looking forward to? They can be big or small, near or far.

That "no-negativity" mindset and focusing on the positives doesn't necessarily come naturally to me. I grimace a bit each time I remember some of my less positive parenting moments.

"Since you can't seem to function in the morning, I'm just going to have to follow you around and keep you on track!" I announced to my oldest son, who was now in third grade. Every time he got distracted, I'd bark out his next task like a drill sergeant. "Put down that book and put *on* your socks!" "It's NOT time to play. GO brush your teeth!" My son became more frustrated, anxious, and angry as the morning wore on... so did I. I was putting all my focus on what he was doing wrong. This is one of many less than proud parenting moments I look back on. I remember clearly how frustrated and fed up I felt with my son. As a third grader, I expected him to be able to navigate through his morning routine more independently. Every time I thought he was on track, getting ready

93

for the day, I would find him distracted, reading a book or back in bed. *He needs a "handler" to keep him on track*, I'd think to myself. Since multiple gentle reminders weren't working, I thought I needed to come down with a firmer approach for him to "shape up." What a game changer for my kids (and for me) when I got deliberate about focusing on the positives in my Parenting Marathons.

Fantastic Five

During your Parenting Marathon, have you found yourself getting stuck in the negative cycle? If so, you aren't alone. Take a deep breath and give yourself grace. Parenting is hard, and when our kids are struggling or exhibiting challenging behaviors, it takes a toll on us. Start with this simple exercise today. Think about five things that your child is doing well. Then, make sure to comment on them to your son or daughter. I have been in Parenting Marathons where it is very hard to think of even one or two things. If you are struggling to think of five, then broaden your scope. Think about their interactions with neighbors or friends, their willingness to get on the school bus without drama, loving affection they give a family pet, putting away their shoes in the proper spot rather than leaving them on the kitchen floor, turning in a homework assignment on time, or a talent in any area such as art, music, athletics, drama, debate, or problem solving. Don't toss all the Fantastic Fives at your child at once. Sprinkle them over the next few days. Make sure your five things are sincere–kids see straight through false compliments–and be mindful that your tone of voice and body language match the kind words. There is no room for sarcasm here. When your daughter happens to put her backpack on its hook rather than on the floor, she will not feel loved if you say with an eye roll, "Well, it's about time you found that hook! Good job." Instead you could say, "Thanks for hanging that up where it belongs. I'm lucky to have such a big kid who helps keep her things in order." Add a hug or a high five and you've given your child a huge gift! Her little action was seen and appreciated! All children value and need words of encouragement.

Your child is worthy of your love regardless of the things he does or doesn't do, so affirm that he is loved just for being himself. Then, be ruthless about finding positive things to recognize. Catch him doing things well. "Mike, I really like how you found something to play with in the kitchen near me while I finish dinner." "Joan, you are always so dependable when it comes to waking up on time. That is one of your strengths, good job." "Kevin, you are so good at playing with your little brother. Thank you for being so much fun!" "Ruby, I can really see how much work you put into that school project. You made a really interesting poster board with the information you learned. Thanks for sharing it with me." The more difficult the Parenting Marathon you are in, the harder you need to focus on the positives.

Look for those times that your child makes a good decision with a situation that they usually struggle with. I mentioned briefly about how the morning noise bothered my daughter. She was great at getting up on time for school but tended to wake up grumpy and was likely to snap at a parent or sibling in the way. This started our day off with hurt feelings and could send the person who got snapped at into a meltdown. I put on my "parent detective hat" and asked her about what would help her in the mornings. She identified that the noise of her siblings and being asked questions by parents first thing in the morning made her feel really irritated. Together we came up with the idea that she could eat her breakfast at the little table in our sunroom (with a door that closes to shut out the noise of the morning). I made a conscious choice in sorting through my feelings on this plan. I fought back feeling like this represented a rejection of me or of family life. I confronted my inner fears that whispered to me that this was a sign I was doing a bad job as a mom; I couldn't wave my wand and make happy family breakfast moments happen on a daily basis. After sorting through my fears and putting it into perspective with a little self-talk ("I'm not a failure as a mom, I'm looking at each child's unique needs"), I chose to see her side, validate her feelings, and give her the space in the mornings that she requested. After that talk, when she would come for breakfast looking grumpy and take off with her food into the sunroom, shutting the door behind her, I would remember to compliment her later on giving herself the time and space she needed to settle into the morning.

There are lots of ways to share your fantastic five with your child. Go simple or get creative!

Here are just a few ideas to get you started:

- Tell him in words as soon as you observe something positive.

- At bedtime, review the day with her and share positive things you noticed.

- Cut out paper hearts or stars (or just use sticky notes). Every so often write a positive thing you noticed on the paper and tape it to his door.

- Add a note to her lunch box or inside her laptop for her to find.

- Send a text or email.

- Highlight one positive thing about each of your kids while you sit down for a family meal.

Your Turn:

1. Make your fantastic five list for each of your children and plan to share them.

2. Make a fantastic five list for your spouse or partner if you have one. Find a way to share them.

Words of Growth:

The running journal I started in my first year of running became a tangible record of progress. I could look back on it and see signs of growth in my running. It is so powerful to be recognized for the growth we've made, in any area. At the end of my second year of running with my local group of women, we had our annual celebration. It was a time to socialize, laugh, and see each other dressed up in something other than running clothes and tennis shoes!

Part of the evening was for awards. These weren't awards in the typical sense, like MVP or most miles run in a year. One award was called the "tree hugger" and went to a wonderful woman who discovered a huge love of running in the woods. The "strong-momma" award went to two women who came back into running after having babies. The award for "Gazelle-the woman who made running look effortless" was announced and it went to me! ME?! Me, who used to purposefully steer the running conversations to the others because I couldn't run, breath, *and* talk. As I went up to get my award, it dawned on me that I *could* run and have a full conversation now. I hadn't noticed that sign of growth in myself until I got the Gazelle award.

Where have you seen growth in your kids? Growth usually takes time and often occurs in small, easy to miss increments. It's sort of like the day you notice your son's pants are so short that he's showing off 2" of ankle. Did that just happen? One day at church as I was getting my family registered, my oldest son, now 14 years old, asked me a question from across the hallway. One of the youth leaders had been on a break, and hadn't seen him in about two months. The leader was shocked at how deep my son's voice had gotten. I hadn't realized until that moment what a change had taken place right in front of me. As attention was called to his manly voice and rapidly growing height, my son beamed at being recognized for these areas of growth.

Of course, growth in our kids is so much more than just the physical changes. They are growing in so many ways, but it can be easy to miss if we don't make an effort to look for the growth and call attention to it. We do something powerful when we notice how they are maturing and we tell them about it!

That year of homeschooling that I shared about earlier, ended up being full of challenges. We started out the year with just a little learning and lots of breaks to play relationship building games. I had a vision of learning being fun and manageable. We kept subject work short, and I pretended to be a different teacher with a unique personality for each of her subjects. "Mr. Math" was like a mathematics coach, encouraging and energetic, full of high fives for the work she did. "Miss Spelling" wore glasses and scarves and talked like a fussy old librarian. She was sort of No Nonsense, but with a kind grandmother-like heart. We incorporated activities like cooking and outdoor adventures into our week. I devoted my days to her education and included our youngest child in our activities after his short preschool class. My heart to help her, time and dedication to her education, and unconditional love for her was not enough to make our homeschooling successful. Every subject was a struggle and each day brought out waves of difficult behaviors.

It took us forever to accomplish a few math problems or a spelling lesson. It was clear that she was frustrated and discouraged. As her stress level ramped up, so did the anger and aggression. The year carried on and I began to feel like I was trapped. No one else saw the explosions that happened after simple statements like "join me on the couch to read." One particularly shocking moment came during reading time on a normal homeschool day. She had read a word incorrectly which commonly led her to feel frustrated that the book "made no sense." I gently corrected the word, hoping we could continue. But it was like a switch had been flipped.

It was seemingly simple little moments like that that could set things off. She was mad and wanted to quit reading. I encouraged her to get to the end of the page and we would take a break. Wrong answer. The anger turned into her screaming directly in my face. I couldn't help her calm down. Nothing I did was right. As she ramped up, her volume reached ear splitting decibels, and she tried to twist my arm that held the book. My husband was home that day from work and had been working in the garage on a project. He unexpectedly entered the house humming to himself. Upon hearing him enter, our daughter extinguished her rage in the blink of an eye and stood looking at me, frozen. It was like she had switched off a light switch on her meltdown. One moment she was screaming and lashing out, and the next she was absolutely silent.

I learned a lot that year, as both her mom and as her homeschool teacher. One of the take-aways for me was learning to watch for small signs of growth and celebrate them. I'll admit, I tend to see the ¾ of a job that's not done, rather than tune into the ¼ of the job that's done. If I ask my daughter to clean up her room, and she picks up the books, but leaves clothes, art supplies, and the tiny bits of shredded paper on the floor, my eyes go to the mess that's left much more automatically than to the books lined up on the shelf. It really takes training to look for the positives, the growth, the part of the task that is done. Acknowledging what's done well, and highlighting the strengths before bringing up the parts that fall short, makes a huge difference.

I was becoming a dedicated student myself, learning everything I could about trauma, behavior, attachment, neurodiversity, learning differences, and parenting. I was adding to my parenting toolbox and putting my new skills into practice. As the homeschooling year progressed and things started to improve in our home, I got better and better at seeing the positives and verbalizing the growth. I found myself saying things like, "I could tell you were really frustrated about your reading, but you didn't scream. I see how much you're growing!" That might seem like a ridiculous statement, but it acknowledges the growing self-control and frustration tolerance she was building. She beamed under each acknowledgment of her gains.

Your Turn:

1. Is it easier for you to see the part of the chore that's not finished, or the part that your child accomplished?

2. Do you tend to expect your child to learn more from you correcting them when they are wrong, or from you recognizing them when they do something right?

Step Seven Quick Glance:

- Focus on the positives and avoid getting stuck in negativity.

- The Fantastic Five is a simple practice of thinking of five things your child is doing well, then sharing those things with your child over the next several days.

- Look for opportunities to share words of growth with your child along the way. Growth can happen gradually at times. Recognizing small steps and progress will brighten your child's day!

"Comparison is the thief of joy."

- THEODORE ROOSEVELT

Step Eight:
AVOID THE COMPARISON GAME

If you are involved in any sport or activity from running to playing piano, from tennis to quilting, it's unlikely that you are the VERY, VERY best in the world in that activity. As a runner, I'm faster than some and slower than some. During a race, I can always look around and see someone whose running looks more effortless or who is faster than I am. On the flip side, I can look around and see another runner going at a slower pace or struggling more than me at that moment.

And here's what I've learned: **It's not Fast or Slow; it's that you Go!**

Another person's pace or race doesn't change the race set out for *me*.

One of the lessons I learned training for a marathon is the concept of "run your own race." Your race is unique to you. No one can run it for you. Comparing your race to another person's isn't going to help. In fact, getting overly preoccupied with someone else's race is liable to increase your stress and decrease your joy during your own run. We each have our own race to run. We can and should support and encourage each other while we run our race, but we *each* need to run. Even if a runner chooses to run an entire marathon with a running buddy, supporting and encouraging each other as they go, keeping the same pace and making memories together, maybe grabbing some selfies along the way, they each still need to run their own race. The same is true in parenting. We need to run our own race.

So how do we run our own race in our Parenting Marathons?

Start with Acceptance

This Parenting Marathon *is* happening. It's happening and it is going to be hard... marathons are always hard. It's also unique. There has never been another Parenting Marathon exactly like yours. Even if you have a co-parent, a partner or spouse, his/her experience with this marathon is different from yours. Seek out the support you need, but no-one can run this race for you. Accepting that you're in a Parenting Marathon, a challenging and unique parenting season, helps you tap into your inner strength. Accepting is the opposite of hiding our heads in the sand and hoping things will blow over. Accepting is taking an honest look at the situation you're in, not trying to ignore the challenges, see them through rose-colored glasses, or downplay the situation. Acceptance can be hard.

Take the examples of two different moms that I worked with. Both came to me concerned about their child's out-of-control behaviors. Both kids demanded things from their parents and if they didn't get their way, with a quick enough response, they would fly into a rage, destroying property and at times becoming aggressive with their moms. Both of these kids experienced forms of early life trauma and had been struggling at home and school.

The first mom who I'll call Joan, embraced the idea of accepting the current situation and the challenges they were facing. They were in an extremely difficult spot; she was worn out and had been feeling very alone in her Parenting Marathon. Her two children had experienced trauma in the home by verbal and sometimes physical abuse by another adult. As a result, her older son's nervous system was on hyper alert, and he quickly became dysregulated over seemingly small things. They were in crisis mode. One of the most beautiful things about Joan was her ability to be honest and open about the struggles she was experiencing parenting her child, her need for help, and her desire for change. Her acceptance of their starting point and willingness to seek support was a crucial first step on a journey to improved relationships and behaviors in the home.

The other mom who I'll call Wendy, was also worn out and exhausted from managing so many challenging behaviors from her teenage son. Her Parenting Marathon had lasted for over a decade and she was understandably feeling very burnt out. It was much harder for Wendy to make progress and lead her family towards healing and growth, though, because Wendy struggled to accept the severity of the behaviors. When we attempted to talk about a safety plan to keep her from getting physically hurt by her son, she said, "Well, if I just give him what he wants, things calm down." This exhausted and well-intentioned mom often lived in fear of her child's outbursts. If the house didn't have the snack he wanted, he would demand that she go and buy it for him. If that didn't happen quickly enough, she was liable to get hurt. Struggling to accept the severity of the situation they were in meant it was also hard for her to accept help. By embracing the idea that things "aren't so bad," or that "nothing could make a positive difference," she faced a significant roadblock to progress.

Accepting doesn't change the reality. It doesn't make the reality better or worse. It's simply deciding to see the challenge for what it really is. What is the reality of your situation? It doesn't have to be as severe as Wendy and Joan's challenges with children who quickly became aggressive and even dangerous. Maybe for you accepting looks like taking an honest look at a broken relationship you have with your teenager. Maybe as a step-parent, acceptance looks like acknowledging that your step-child doesn't trust you yet, and building that trust and relationship will take time.

Your Turn:

1. What is an area of acceptance you want to work on?

Block it Out

Let's face it, as parents there is always going to be someone we can point to who seems to be doing better than we are: the couple who seems to have it all together when they parade their perfect family into church in matching outfits; that mom whose child is the valedictorian of the world and prom queen as well; the neighbor who has perfect hair and nails, manages a full-time corporate job, all while raising three delightful kids who are basically like robots when it comes to listening; the dad whose kids cling to his every word and think he walks on water. Social media is flooded with images of perfect families performing perfectly. Social media is like a highlight reel. When I think about what gets included in the one family photo album I make each year, it's the highlights: pictures of everyone's birthday celebrations, Christmas, athletic events, fun summer memories, visits with grandparents, etc. We don't tend to publicize or memorialize the rocky moments: the mouthy child or defiant teen, the speeding tickets, missed curfews, failing grades, or disastrously messy bedrooms. It's normal and good to want to remember and celebrate the good moments. Think about the previous chapter on focusing on the positives. The problem can come when we compare our Parenting Marathon with another parent's journey based on these few glimpses of their highlight reel. That sort of comparison is bound to make you feel like you're falling short, missing the mark, or just plain failing. But *you* are not failing. You are showing up every day doing the work, learning as you go, and making a positive difference in the lives of your kids. Resist the urge to compare your family or your Parenting Marathon to another person's. Run your own race, support and encourage others, and leave comparison to the amateurs. If or when you start to compare your journey to someone else's, be kind to yourself, but firm. Remind yourself, "My marathon is unique. I'm running a Parenting Marathon that's never been run before."

"Run the Mile You're In"

During my first half marathon there was a sizable uphill climb early on, and I remember commenting about another, even bigger hill we would encounter later on in the course. The friend running with me said, "Remember, run the mile you're in." I laughed... What on earth did that mean? How could I run anything else but the mile I'm in? She (able to talk while running fast and make it look easy) explained that in a long race, it's best to focus on the current mile, rather than start to worry about what mile 12 or 20 is going to be like. We can just take care of the mile we are *in*. Sounds a lot like parenting, right? We may start to worry about mile 26, but right now, we need to run the mile we're in. Bring your focus back to the present. In the words of Lao Tzu and Dana Parisi:

Depression is a focus on the past.

Anxiety is a focus on the future.

The solution is to stay in the present... run the mile you're in.

Running the mile you're in keeps you focused on the present. When we are present in the current moment, we worry less about the future and don't let the past control us.

Your Turn:

1. Do you tend to look around and compare your Parenting Marathon to someone else's?

2. Do you tend to dwell in the past, regretting decisions, second guessing things, or reliving moments?

3. Do you tend to focus too far into the future and get stressed with the unknowns?

Step Eight Quick Glance:

- Your Parenting Marathon is unique! Comparing it to another person's race is a trap you want to avoid. Block it out, and run your own race.

- Take an honest look at the current situation you're in, and accept it for the challenging endurance event that it is.

- Focus on the present rather than dwelling on the past or worrying about the future. Run the mile you're in.

"There is no such thing as a perfect parent. So just be a real one."

- SUE ATKINS

Step Nine:

DON'T WALLOW IN GUILT OVER SET-BACKS OR PERCEIVED FAILURES

Iremember feeling like my marathon training was going so smoothly. My task-oriented brain loves a training sheet, and I found joy in checking off each run. The miles were slowly getting longer. The Wisconsin winter weather wasn't holding me back... I was succeeding! I worked my way through a 16-mile training run in blowing snow and 20 degree weather. This run consisted of four laps around a four-mile loop of well-maintained bike paths in town known as the "wintermission." These trails got high priority for snow removal, a city plan to have an inviting place for people to get outside in the winter. This 16-mile run was the longest run of my life so far! A new PR (personal record)! It was hard. I felt tired. My legs felt sore. It was tempting to quit after the second loop, and then again after the third, but I persevered. I finished the 16 miles. I probably didn't stretch at all after that run. I'm sure I started getting cold on the drive home, jumped into the shower, and then on to the rest of my day. That run was checked off my list! The next morning, however, something was seriously wrong. My right foot felt like I had a tack in my heel. I couldn't put any pressure on the heel of my foot without feeling like I was driving the tack in deeper. I hobbled around and looked for an explanation. There wasn't anything there that I could see, but something was preventing me from putting my weight on that poor heel. When I did, the pain went straight through my body. I was injured! NOOOO!

Every runner dreads injuries. Not only couldn't I run, I could hardly walk. I limped around my house, helping my kids get ready in the morning. Every task seemed to take forever. My running training plan came to a screeching halt. It took me two full weeks of rest and care to feel like I might be on the road to recovery.

I felt terrible, both physically and emotionally. Feelings of guilt that I hadn't "trained properly" plagued me. I also felt guilty that my "little hobby" of running was now negatively affecting my whole life. I had never meant for it to interfere with raising my kids. Everytime I walked, it hurt. I couldn't walk the dog with my kids or play with them on the trampoline we set up as soon as the yard had a spot clear of snow. I avoided driving if I could because even that hurt. I felt like a failure. Plenty of people train for a marathon. Why couldn't I do it?

"Failures" or setbacks are part of the journey in running and in parenting. When training for a long race with my friends, there is the understanding that everyone is going to have at least one really rough or even terrible long run leading up to the big race. In fact, when someone has that really bad long run (they feel winded, their legs feel like lead, or they feel slow and tired the whole time), we shrug it off and even celebrate. "Hey, you got your 'bad run' out of the way! Better to have a bad training run than a bad race day."

In Parenting Marathons, there are going to be "bad runs." They will look different for each of us, but it's inevitable that each of us WILL have bad runs. Maybe you blew up at your kid when they were acting silly at the table and spilled a glass of milk. Maybe you lost your cool over something and sent your daughter off to bed crying. Maybe your middle schooler said something horrible to you and hurt your heart (kids have an incredible radar to find the most sensitive target for their words when they're upset). Maybe you and your teen had a giant fight about clothes, curfew, or friends. Perhaps you said things you regret. Maybe your child is making big mistakes that you can't protect him from. There are so many versions of a "bad run" when it comes to parenting. Some parenting "bad runs" are short painful moments; others are much longer seasons of mistakes. Regardless of the specifics of your most recent "bad run," you're not alone. You *are* going to make mistakes. Your child *is* going to make mistakes. You *are* going to have setbacks, false starts, and failures along the way. Some of our failures make us want to stick our heads in the sand and hide, but we can't run the race before us with our head in the sand. We need to have tools to shake off the guilt and feelings of failure so we can get back in the race.

One memorable parenting low for me was a huge mommy tirade I launched at my oldest child when he was in 7th grade. He was attending a unique science-based, public charter school at a nature reserve. His classroom was a one room meeting area in between twin towers that housed giant telescopes for the nature center. His middle school was literally a one room schoolhouse. My son had a long history of losing things. Ever since he was old enough to have things he cared about, he was losing things. As a little kid, he frequently lost his favorite stuffed animal, a Bernese Mountain Dog named Special Puppy. He would lose one shoe to most sets of shoes. Mittens went through his hands like water, even when we attempted to tie them into his coat with string. As a 7th grader, he had recently lost several things at school, including his jacket and his wallet (which he didn't need to take to school in the first place). On this particularly memorable day, he finished up school and walked to the parking lot where I waited to drive him home. As he approached the car with his familiar loping walk, I immediately noticed that he didn't have his backpack. I calmly (I think...) asked about it.

Me: "Hey, where's your backpack?"

Him: "No idea, it totally disappeared."

That's how things were when he lost items. In his mind, they just vanished out of thin air and would never ever be able to be found. He had made premature peace with the opinion that things just slipped away from him, and that was just how it was. Nothing could be done about it.

Me: "Go back to the building and look for it."

Him: "Okay, but I looked everywhere already."

118

He was gone another 10 minutes or so before I followed him across the wide open lawn and into the single room building that held his middle school. Not a lot of possible places for a backpack to hide, but just like he said, it wasn't there. No sign of his backpack. His teachers agreed with him that they hadn't seen it. I asked him to search the bathroom, which was the only other room in the small space. No backpack. His teachers shrugged; he shrugged. I kept my cool as we walked back to the van (backpack-less). Then, as we started driving home... I let him have it.

"HOW COULD YOU LOSE YOUR BACKPACK IN A ONE ROOM SCHOOLHOUSE?! You go to school in a SINGLE ROOM! There is NO place to lose a backpack. What on earth do you do with your things? Why do you keep losing EVERYTHING? This is the third thing THIS WEEK you've lost at school! You're driving me nuts!" And on and on I went for the 18-minute drive home. I'm sure I said something about his ability to lose his own head if it wasn't attached. He shrank in his chair, not bothering to justify his forgetfulness and just let me rant. Sigh. By the time we got home, we both felt pretty awful.

Later that day, once I recovered my calm, I went and apologized for yelling at him. I was still upset that he lost his backpack, but I knew I had handled it poorly. Yelling at him didn't help find the missing backpack, and it eroded our relationship. I gave him a hug with my apology and then sat with him.

"Can you walk me through your day at school? What did you do when you got to class? Where do you normally put your things?"

He answered, but it didn't shed any light on the situation.

"Did you do anything outside of your classroom yesterday?"

My gentler approach paid off. He told me they spent almost the whole day at school, except for the end when they went to the river.

"How did you get to the river? Did you walk?" I asked.

"No, we rode the bus... Hey! That's where my backpack is! I thought the bus was taking me all the way home, so I took my backpack along. I bet I left it under a seat," he said. And of course, that's where he found it the next day.

The bottom line is, you are going to make mistakes in your parenting journey. You will have great moments that you look back on and feel like you hit a parental PR (personal record). In those moments, you will feel like you were at your best, you used your parenting tools well, and positive things happened. There will also be moments where you totally "hit a wall," when you have a parenting "bad run," mess up, lose your cool, or regret what you said or did, or what you didn't say or do. Wallowing in feelings of guilt can get us stuck. And being stuck is the opposite of growing. Instead, own your "bad runs" by owning your mistakes, apologize when appropriate, take steps to repair the relationship, and get back out there. We want to teach our kids to be resilient, and handle the bumps of life without getting dragged down. We can use these opportunities to model resilience and self-forgiveness.

Your Turn:

1. Without judging yourself, are you currently growing or are you stuck in the Parenting Marathon you're in?

2. What area of guilt or perceived failure do you need to acknowledge in order to move forward?

Step Nine Quick Glance:

- Parenting Marathons will have set backs. You will make mistakes along the way.

- Give yourself grace rather than wallowing in guilt, and continue to learn and grow rather than beating yourself up.

- Own your "bad runs," apologize when appropriate, take steps to repair the relationship, and move forward.

"The journey of a thousand miles must begin with a single step."

- Lao Tzu

Step Ten:

STEP UP TO THE STARTING LINE

Have you ever done a ton of preparation for something like a family trip, a big event, or a work project? Then, when the "big day" comes, despite all your efforts and planning, things still go awry? Give yourself a pep talk, and step up to the starting line anyways!

My marathon training didn't go according to plan. I did *have* a plan, I printed it off and hung it on my wall. I was diligently checking off each run. Then the foot injury happened. I couldn't walk without pain. I focused on rest and recovery and doing any other activity I could do to stay strong physically and mentally. I tried to hold on to my motivation and not get stuck. I lifted weights, stretched, swam, and rode a stationary bike. I iced, foam-rolled, and even tried something called dry needling, where a trained Physical Therapist stuck tiny needles into my calf and the bottom of my foot to relieve tightness (I don't want to talk any more about that... thinking about it makes me squirm). The good news was I was getting better!

During this recovery time, COVID was ramping up, and my early May marathon had just been canceled. Well, we actually got two options: run the race virtually (which means you run it on your own) and record the time, or transfer your race fee to the following year. Although a race fee could be transferred from one year to another, the training couldn't. Despite my two weeks off from running while I recovered, I felt strong and ready to go. I wanted to accomplish this marathon. Since I had never run a marathon before, it didn't really matter to me that I wouldn't have race support or cheering crowds. I was more in it to challenge myself as a runner and grow. No one could run this race for me. It was time for me to step up to the old starting line, even if it was virtual. Actually, since the official race was canceled, my starting line was going to be right out my front door! I picked the following Saturday and told my family and close friends that I was going for it! I was going to run my own course, get the 26.2 miles done, and finish my first marathon.

As I suited up in my kitchen, laced up my running shoes, and stashed gel fuel sources in my pockets, I told myself it was "just another long run... no big deal." There were certainly voices of doubt in my head. "What if I can't do it?" But those voices are rarely helpful and I brushed them off, gave my husband a kiss, and started running. There are parts of that run that are simply a blur in my mind. My course for that first four miles had a nice gradual decline. Running downhill is pretty easy, so I just enjoyed the ride. Then came the familiar four mile "wintermission loop" that I had run so many times during my winter training. After that I met up with one of my experienced running friends, one of the few people that I had told about my plan to run my solo marathon. She had offered to run a 10-mile stretch with me. Her company, encouragement, and confidence made a huge difference in my morale. When I started dragging, she gently reminded me I needed to fuel and drink water. I choked down a gel fuel at her suggestion, and really did feel better quickly.

One foot in front of the other, I kept going. By the time we circled back to her car, I had 8 miles left to go. I hugged my friend, and kept on moving. One more four-mile loop of the wintermission, then the four miles back to my house, and I'd be done. Since I had enjoyed the nice gradual run downhill from my house, I now had to make my way up the hill in order to get home. Something about running hills is that you can barely perceive it when you're going downhill and the work is easier, but you sure notice it going uphill when the challenge is on. (Sometimes parenting is like that, isn't it? We can take it for granted when it's easy, but we take notice when it gets hard!) I distinctly remember the final two miles. I couldn't wait to be done. Running up the last steep part of the hill to get home, I felt like I just needed to walk. My legs were tired, my hips were tight, my feet were sore. Really and truly, it's ok to walk. But to my surprise, walking didn't really feel any better. What I wanted was to be done! Picking up my speed back to a jog made more sense than prolonging this by walking further. My unofficial race course brought me to exactly 26 miles on the bike path across the street from my house. Being a stickler for the rules I had to complete the final .2 miles. One foot in front of the other, .1 mile past my house and then back, and... I did it! 26.2 miles. My exhaustion was paired with feeling accomplished. My husband was waiting for me and took my marathon finish line photo. He and our younger two kids had made me a finisher's medal from a tin can lid and a screen-printed Parisi Marathon t-shirt for my "swag."

When it comes to your Parenting Marathon, no one else can do what you can do. No one else can run the race for you. You are the expert on your child. If you have a co-parent, you have a partner in this marathon, and you each have a unique race to run. You may have a line-up of amazing experts helping support your family, including mental health therapists, parent coaches, school staff, and medical professionals. Maybe you have great family and friends who you can lean on. They are your race supports. They are there to hand you some water or fuel, give you a rest stop if you need it, offer you advice and encouragement and cheer you on. But they can't and won't run the Parenting Marathon for you.

Many times, parents in a Parenting Marathon feel like they have little or no "race support." Parents in extended seasons of struggle can feel too exhausted to keep up with their previous support systems, or they may feel misunderstood, judged, or like they are a burden. Some Parenting Marathons can be very isolating, but *you are not alone*. You know you have a job to do, a race that only you can run. There will be downhill stretches that feel smooth and easy, and uphill stretches that make you want to quit. There will be moments when you feel strong and capable, and moments when you feel like you are not enough... but *you are enough.* You've got what it takes. Lace up those shoes and take on your Parenting Marathon, one step at a time.

Your Turn:

1. Step up to the starting line by reviewing your notes and deciding which 1-3 practical training steps you will start taking. Use this format:

   In order to _____, I will _____.

   Here are just a few examples:

   - In order to simplify schedules, I will keep Sundays free of activities.

   - In order to help my son have less meltdowns, I will start my parent detective notebook and pay attention to what triggers him.

   - In order to focus on the positives, I will make my fantastic five list for each person in my family and start to share it with them.

Step Ten Quick Glance:

- You are the right person to take on this Parenting Marathon, and no one can run this race for you.

- Be confident. You are the expert on your child, and you are not alone. You have what it takes, so step up to the starting line.

"You can't run another person's race for them."

- DANA PARISI

Final Thoughts:
YOUR CHILD'S OWN MARATHON

As parents, we want to see our kids find success. When they struggle, it's painful for us. Sometimes we feel we can predict the future better than our child can, and we would like to help them avoid mistakes. But frankly, we can't run a marathon for our child. As they grow and mature, we also keep maturing in our role. We can provide race support for our kids as they navigate their lives and their own decisions. We can offer guidance, advice, encouragement, even emergency support if needed, but we can't run their race. As we help our kids navigate through their teen years, we are also navigating a slow change in our role and practicing letting them run their own race.

I remember the first time that I really started to realize that I couldn't run a race for my child. The first day of first grade, my son ended up "hanging out" with the principal because he couldn't stop arguing with his teacher. His Montessori class was a combination of first, second, and third grades, and he couldn't accept that the third graders had more privileges in the class than the new first graders. He debated this with his teacher, didn't find her answer satisfying, and wouldn't let the argument go. So, he was "invited" to go chat with the principal. *He* felt fine with the plan, and enjoyed talking with the principal while they played catch in the gym. *I* felt embarrassed. "How many kids get sent to the principal's office the first day of first grade?" I asked my husband, dismayed. I would have been mortified as a child to be sent to the principal's office and wouldn't have considered arguing with my teacher. But my son and I are two unique individuals. He's not merely an extension of myself.

My son saw the classroom situation as an injustice. In his mind, all the classmates should have the same privileges regardless of their age, so this was worth fighting about. If I had been hovering in the background of that argument with his teacher, I would have tried to pull him away and prevent him from getting in trouble. But I'm glad I wasn't there to try to "save" him. I realized that my 6-year-old was his own person, and will make different decisions than I might make. He is going to run his own races. As his race support, I can admire his heart for justice and his willingness to stand up for what he believes is right. I can talk with him about mature ways of navigating differences of opinions and having respect for his teachers. But I can't run the race for any of my kids. Now, as he nears his 18th birthday, I often need to remind myself of my changing role from his manager to his consultant.

As you and your child run your own marathons, I hope these chapters have been helpful, and that you have an action plan you can start implementing right away. Look in the free resources for a printable document to record your next steps. Print it off and post it somewhere like your bathroom mirror, where you'll see it often. Also, keep this book handy for the future Parenting Marathons you encounter. Review these 10-steps and make a new action plan for each challenging situation.

Thank you for letting me be a part of your Parenting Marathon. We are stronger as parents when we are supported and support others. Your story matters. There is always hope for growth. In my toughest Parenting Marathon with my daughter, I remember desperately wanting *her* to get better: to stop having epic meltdowns, to learn to listen, and to be teachable... but that change only happened after I made lots of changes in my own approach. I had to be the change first, before I saw growth and healing in my daughter. You can be the agent of healing and growth in your home. The journey may be hard, but not impossible. You can't complete the race if you don't start. This event is yours to win, so **step up to the starting line**.

Learn How to Work with Me

If you are looking at your reflections from these chapters and find yourself ready for additional support, please reach out to me. I would love to help you define your goals, make a robust self-care plan, plan for common struggles, learn to look for progress, consider where you need to simplify, build your support team, make adjustments to your mindset, look for the positives, avoid the comparison trap and persevere through parent guilt and burnout. YOU can run your Parenting Marathon with strength, endurance, courage and JOY!

Parent coaching with me can provide:

- support, encouragement, and empathy for **you** on this Parenting Marathon

- training to look for the "root causes" of the challenging behaviors and ways to address them

- tools to help you stay calm and help your child calm down from a meltdown

- tips and problem solving for your toughest parenting challenges

- increased empathy and understanding for your child who is struggling

- improved relationship with your child

- next steps to help your child grow

- tools to measure and watch for progress

- improved relationships between siblings in your home

- **hope for the future**

Lives Touched LLC is my small business dedicated to supporting parents and families. I work with all kinds of parents: biological parents, adoptive and foster parents, grandparents raising grandchildren, and kinship parents. Why? Because everyone who is parenting a child is going to go through a marathon and deserves support, encouragement, and resources. I love working with parents who understand the value of getting guidance, as well as those doing their own self-development.

Whether you're interested in self-paced parent coaching programs, group coaching, one-on-one coaching, events, trainings, or you just want to follow along with my emails to get tips, advice, and resources, here are a couple of ways to get started:

1. Access the bonus resources page that I already mentioned. There, you can grab your workbook and free video training, and become a part of my community for even more resources and advice. Go to www.ParentingMarathon.com/resources.

2. Check out my website to see the different options available at www.LivesTouchedCoaching.com/

3. If you're not sure where to start, then it's best if we can have a one-on-one call to discuss your unique situation, and see if or how I can support you. You can schedule that call with myself or my team online at www.LivesTouchedCoaching.com/free-call.

"Dana's 1on1 parent coaching was practical and helpful. Her approach to tackling tricky behavior made so much sense and really helped to restore relationships within our family. We are excited to continue learning more from her and to benefit from her guidance on our parenting journey!"

– AG

"My experience with Parent Coaching was amazing! I was at a point of what felt like a point of no return in my relationship with my child. My parenting skills felt nonexistent. With Dana's help, I was able to breathe again and connect with my child. It's a work in progress on our end but the support I received through Parent Coaching saved us! We are so thankful & feel confident now that we are on a good healthy track."

- SC

"Before meeting with Dana, our life was filled with chaos and meltdowns several times a day. Since I have been able to use and implement the tools that Dana has helped me develop, we are down to 2-3 meltdowns a week. We are able to go places and enjoy life now and not have to worry about what might happen."

- Ann H

ABOUT THE AUTHOR
Dana Parisi

Dana Parisi is Certified Parent Coach and Educational Trainer with a focus on trauma-informed approaches. Her first profession as a Physical Therapist was sparked by her passion for individual and family health and wellness. She graduated from Marquette University with both her B.S and MPT. After starting her career in physical therapy, she spent over a year living and volunteering at Nuestros Pequenos Hermanos (Our

Little Brothers and Sisters) orphanage in Honduras. This experience fueled her passion for children and families, and contributed to her and her husband's decision to adopt two of their children many years later. She and her husband have led several small groups on short-term visits to NPH Honduras to build connections and collaborate. They were given the NPH Friends of the Orphans Volunteer of the Year award in 2013.

Dana and her husband have four children, two biological and two adopted. They live in Altoona, Wisconsin on a small lake. At the time of publishing, their kids range in age from 8 to 17 years old. As a family, they are busy with various sports teams, church activities, and outdoor adventures, as well as starting to tour colleges for their oldest two kids! During their free time, they enjoy outdoor fun in each of the four seasons Wisconsin offers. Downhill and cross-country skiing, biking, kayaking, canoeing, berry picking, hiking, and camping are some of their favorite activities. They enjoy being a bit unusual as a family and don't own a television, which is just the way they like it. Indoor activities they enjoy include games, puzzles, and reading.

After a significant family move for her husband's career, Dana paused her work as a physical therapist, and stayed at home with her kids for several years. During this time, their family grew through two international adoptions, and they traveled to Ethiopia several times. After their second adoption, Dana homeschooled her oldest child for 6th grade, followed the next year by homeschooling her third child for 2nd grade. During those years, she experienced some of the many joys and challenges of homeschooling and has a great appreciation for the work of teachers.

Dana chose to change careers to Parent Coaching and Educational Training after experiencing the benefits of working with a coach herself through some of her biggest Parenting Marathons. Recognizing the beneficial role of having guidance and support through parenting struggles, she completed her dual certification in Parent Coaching and Educational Training through Heart Strong International in 2021, and started her business Lives Touched LLC. Dana works with parents locally, as well as globally through one-on-one coaching, group coaching, webinars, presentations, and self-paced courses.

As a Certified Educational Trainer, she has had opportunities to work with schools, churches, and nonprofit organizations by giving presentations on various topics including trauma, connection, and behavior.

Dana has a passion for her community. As a volunteer at her local school district, she serves as the District Family Engagement Liaison, helping connect parents and educators of students who have additional needs to appropriate resources. Dana also serves on the advisory board for the Wisconsin Adoption and Permanency Support program, which provides support to Wisconsin adoptive and guardianship families, birth parents, and adult adoptees. She and her three oldest children serve regularly at their church, Jacob's Well, supporting the children's and family ministry.

Dana discovered a love of long-distance running in 2018 when she joined Moms on the Run, a structured fitness program for women of all ages. In an attempt to keep running through the long Wisconsin winter, she trained for her first half-marathon, which she ran in the spring of 2019. At the time of publishing, Dana has completed four half-marathons, one team marathon relay, and two full marathons. She has been a coach for Moms on the Run for four years and loves to support other women in their fitness journeys and goals. She's currently working on learning some basic mountain biking skills to be able to enjoy the trails with her kids.

When she's not spending time with her family, working, or running, Dana is usually enjoying time with friends, reading, or organizing family photos albums. She also loves traveling and visiting National Parks.

The Ideal Speaker for Your Next Event or Webinar!

Any school, non-profit, or business that wants to help parents, educators, or staff be prepared to support children needs to hire Dana for a keynote and/or workshop training!

A Few of Dana's Keynote Presentations:

- Compassion and Connection in the Classroom

- Meltdown Management

- Parent Detective: Unraveling Challenging Behaviors and Building Self-Regulation Skills

- Persevering Through Caregiver Guilt and Burnout

To book Dana to speak, contact:

Lives Touched LLC

LivesTouchedCoaching.com

LivesTouchedCoaching@gmail.com

www.ingramcontent.com/pod-product-compliance
Lightning Source LLC
Chambersburg PA
CBHW071755090426
42737CB00012B/1833